THE DILEMMA OF PRIESTLESS SUNDAYS

James Dallen
With a foreword by Bishop William E. McManus

LTP Liturgy Training Publications

ACKNOWLEDGMENTS

Copyright © 1994, Archdiocese of Chicago: Liturgy Training Publications, 1800 North Hermitage Avenue, Chicago IL 60622-1101; 1-800-933-1800; FAX 1-800-933-7904. All rights reserved.

This book was edited by David A. Lysik, with the assistance of Deborah Bogaert and Ron Lewinski. It was designed by Kerry Perlmutter, typeset by Mark Hollopeter in Bembo and Futura, and printed by BookCrafters. The index was prepared by Mary Laur.

Library of Congress Cataloging-in-Publication Data
Dallen, James.
　The dilemma of priestless Sundays/James Dallen; with a foreword by William E. McManus.
　　p. cm.
　Includes bibliographical references and index.
　ISBN 1-56854-042-6
　1. Catholic Church — Liturgy without a priest — United States. 2. Catholic Church — United States — Clergy — Appointment, call, and election. 3. Christian leadership — Catholic Church. I. Title.
BX1970.D27 1994
264'.02 — dc20   94-31579
　　　　　　　　　　　　　　　　　　　　　　　　　　　CIP

ISBN 1-56854-042-6
DP/SUN

CONTENTS

FOREWORD

by Bishop William E. McManus

The U.S. church, particularly its bishops, are confronting a difficult dilemma. If a priest is not available for Sunday Mass in a parish church, should the parish church be closed, or should permission be given for a lay person (or a deacon) to conduct a ritual called "Sunday Worship in the Absence of a Priest" (SWAP)?

Closing a church usually provokes a storm of protest. "Without our church," the parishioners say, "our parish is dead. We will not let the bishop or anyone else kill it. Somehow we will keep our parish alive."

Relying on SWAP often seems to be a satisfactory alternative. The parish community continues without an ordained priest in residence but with a competent pastoral leader or administrator in charge. All normal parish services are provided, except that on most Sundays, SWAP, rather than the Mass, constitutes the parish's worship. Parishes that use SWAP sometimes are called "priestless," unintentionally insinuating that no priest, not even Jesus Christ, is essential for Sunday worship pleasing to God.

"What are they SWAPing for?" asks Father James Dallen in this scholarly, copiously documented and pleasantly readable treatise on the doctrinal, theological and pastoral ramifications of SWAP.

Parishes without an ordained priest to celebrate the Sunday eucharist, the author says, break with our Roman Catholic tradition. We believe that "Do this in memory of me" was an explicit request that is fulfilled only in the complete celebration of the eucharist. Vatican II reaffirmed this doctrine by declaring: "No Christian community can be built without roots and foundations in the celebration of the most holy eucharist."

The author predicts that, over a period of time, priestless parishes will see little need for a permanent priest pastor. Their expectations of priesthood will be met by a "circuit-riding" ordained man who comes occasionally to replenish the parish's supply of consecrated bread for communion services, to hear a few confessions and, as needed, to anoint the sick.

Priestless parishes will become "eucharistless" communities whose worship is limited to services of the word with a devotional communion service added. The sacrifice of the Mass will disappear. Non-ordained pastors of priestless parishes will feel more and more "deprived of ordination" when they see their parish's sacramental life deteriorate to the detriment of the Christian community they are trying to develop. A circuit-riding priest and a discontented, non-priest pastor will not make a good leadership team. Priestless parishes without Sunday Mass will also become isolated from the diocesan and universal church. Declining attendance at SWAP will aggravate this.

Acknowledging that the shortage of priests is a critical problem in the contemporary church, Fr. Dallen nevertheless maintains that SWAP, seen from the perspective of traditional doctrine and sound theology, is "a more radical departure from tradition than changing the ordination discipline" that allows only male celibates to be ordained to the priesthood. This book, however, is not a polemic advocating the ordination of women and optional celibacy. Nor does the author's emphasis on the role of the assembly in the eucharistic celebration imply that he favors letting the assembly choose anyone it wants (a practice in the church's earliest centuries) to preside at the eucharist. But SWAP is no remedy for the dearth of priests — it might even make the situation worse by unintentionally demeaning ordained priesthood's function in today's church.

Many historical precedents and developments cited by the author add credibility to his well-founded fear about SWAP's potential for disaster in the contemporary church. If it is true that "the law of praying is the law of believing," then SWAP, both in theory and in practice, may undermine if not destroy Catholics' faith in the eucharist.

If this book had been available at the time, the National Conference of Catholic Bishops might have delayed its widely publicized approval of SWAP. Perhaps those bishops who read it now will proceed cautiously in granting permission for SWAP in their dioceses.

INTRODUCTION

A growing population and a diminishing number of clergy have put the Catholic church squarely between two needs deeply embedded in its tradition: the need of a faith community to celebrate the Lord's Supper on the Lord's Day and the need of that community for a priest to preside at the celebration of the eucharist. The consequence of this is that while an increasing number of Catholic communities are called to keep holy the Lord's Day, they cannot do so in the traditional Catholic fashion. They cannot celebrate the eucharist because their pastoral leader is not a priest.

The situation is not new. Throughout history, communities have been deprived of the eucharist by persecution, oppression, isolation, a clergy shortage or some other factor. In Chapter One, "Communities Without the Eucharist," we will examine how some past communities responded and how they were affected by the situation. American Methodism, an offspring of eucharistic revival within the Church of England, provides a particularly striking parallel to postconciliar Catholicism.

The past, of course, has no monopoly on instances of eucharistic deprivation. In modern times, most Christians in mission territory have been "eucharistically underprivileged" due to a lack of priests. As a consequence, missionaries from the time of Francis Xavier (1506–1552) to the present have had to find ways for new faith communities to gather for worship, even without the eucharist.[1] They realized that the church must gather in order to be church. But in an age when the eucharist belonged to the priest and people's participation was largely limited to attendance and occasional communion, the need to gather *for eucharist* went unnoticed. Missionaries sometimes even kept catechesis on the eucharist to a minimum because it was unnecessary and largely useless knowledge.

The rediscovery of the role of the eucharist in the life of the church has led to a twofold recognition: Young churches cannot mature without the eucharist,[2] and they must reach the point where they can provide for their own ministerial needs.[3] Yet the process has been slow, with new churches often remaining dependent for a long time on ministers from older churches.

Celebration of the eucharist has been rare, possible only on the infrequent occasions when a priest has been available.

Communities in both the past and the present have hungered for the eucharist without the possibility of satisfaction. What is new today is that *long-established* churches find themselves in a parallel and steadily worsening situation due to the lack of priests. In Austria, for example, the number of priestless parishes tripled between 1950 and 1976. In 1982, over 22,000 parishes in France were administered by a nonresident priest, and others had no priest.[4] As a consequence, communities have been forced to find a replacement for the usual Sunday eucharist.[5]

In the United States, the situation is especially problematic because Catholics accustomed to a certain level of priestly service seem unwilling to accept a reduction.[6] Yet the statistics are clear. The number of available priests relative to the U.S. Catholic population has been steadily declining since the early 1940s[7] — well before the Second Vatican Council — and will continue to do so for the foreseeable future. In 1942, when the ratio of priests to parishioners was at its best, there was one priest for every 617 Catholics. The projection is that in 2005 there will be one priest for every 2200 Catholics. After an analysis of diocesan clergy statistics for the years 1966 – 1985, Richard A. Schoenherr and Lawrence A. Young have projected that the number of diocesan priests will be reduced by 40 percent, from 35,000 in 1966 to 21,000 in 2005, while the Catholic population will have grown from 45 million to 74 million in the same period.[8] U.S. Catholics, like Catholics in most of the world, will have fewer clergy and less priestly ministry. The consequences are already being felt: In 1982 there were 843 parishes without a resident pastor; in 1992 there were 2047 such parishes.

The reduction in the number of available priests has consequences for the Sunday liturgy because Catholic tradition and discipline require that a priest preside at the eucharist. As a solution, many writers have called for alternatives to the present ordination discipline, including the ordination of married men and the ordination of women. In an even more radical departure from Catholic tradition, some writers have advocated lay presiders at the eucharist. More conservatively, episcopal conferences[9] as well as individual bishops[10] have issued guidelines concerning parish staffing and worship alternatives. The Congregation for Divine Worship has also done so,[11] stressing the "substitutional character of these celebrations"[12] and the need to keep them from coming to be seen as "normative."[13] Yet such policies leave the impression that some substitute for the celebration of the eucharist has been accepted as necessary and will become increasingly common in years to come — itself a radical change! The pragmatic solution adopted in many locales without available clergy is that members of such communities either travel elsewhere to celebrate the eucharist or gather as a community for "Sunday Worship in the Absence of a Priest."

Sunday Worship in the Absence of a Priest — SWAP — is the phrase used in the subtitle of the statement by the U.S. Bishops' Committee on the Liturgy, *Gathered in Steadfast Faith*. It denotes the liturgical celebration of communities which, for lack of a priest, cannot celebrate the eucharist on the Lord's Day but must instead substitute another form of worship. Generally, when possible, SWAP parallels the traditional Sunday celebration of word and sacrament with a combined word and communion service. We will examine this phenomenon in Chapter Two, "Sunday Worship in the Absence of a Priest." The history of communion outside Mass will provide a foundation for analyzing the contemporary communion service and its relationship to the eucharist.

The acronym SWAP highlights that an exchange is indeed taking place. What are we SWAPing for? And why, for what purpose, and what are we receiving in exchange, are the unacknowledged questions. Are communities, which have no choice in the matter, fully aware of what they are giving up and getting in return? Are church officials, who are making the choice, fully conscious of the path on which they are taking the church? Are both groups aware of what is at stake for communities and for the church in the policy decisions that are being made in the current critical situation?

The central questions concern the consequences for parish communities and for the church if SWAP becomes an acceptable replacement for the Sunday eucharist. Does it make a difference whether a community celebrates the eucharist or whether its members receive communion at SWAP? Will the absence of the eucharist alter the church's sense of identity and mission? How will Catholic spirituality, always sacramental in character, be affected if it lacks the eucharist as its foundation? Can the church continue on the direction it set for itself at the Second Vatican Council without celebrating the Lord's Supper on the Lord's Day?

The church makes the eucharist and the eucharist makes the church. This statement makes so fundamental a claim that nothing would so radically change the church as losing its sacramental foundation in eucharistic celebration. For this reason, we need to look carefully at what this SWAP entails and ask whether alternatives might be preferable. Careful consideration of available choices is crucial to shaping the character of the church as it enters the third millennium. Doing nothing, tolerating an ersatz eucharist, is a more radical departure from the Catholic tradition of Sunday eucharist than any alternative that has been proposed.

This book will be devoted in great part to a study of the ecclesiological concerns that emerge as the eucharist and SWAP are compared. Chapter Three will examine the role of the eucharist in establishing and maintaining ecclesial communion. Chapter Four will focus on the unique character of the eucharistic celebration for establishing and maintaining Christian identity. Chapter Five will deal with the most sensitive issues: the significance of ordination for pastoral ministry and the role of the ordained priest. Finally, Chapter Six will draw together the likely implications of SWAP for Catholic spirituality, for the church's sense of identity and for its sense of mission. The central question throughout is: What effect will the failure to obey the Lord's command have on the community of disciples?

I wish to express my gratitude to colleagues in the 1993 Liturgical Spirituality Workgroup of the North American Academy of Liturgy and to colleagues and students in the Religious Studies Department of Gonzaga University for their discussion and critique of the ideas[14] and paper[15] out of which this book has grown. I also give thanks to Saint Ann's Parish in Spokane, Washington, whose people are committed to being a full-time parish without a full-time priest. The people of Saint Ann's have welcomed me as a member, a minister and an occasional presider at the eucharist. Their celebration of the eucharist as the source and summit of life and ministry nourishes me. Their willingness to try new paths assures me that the risen Lord will continue to draw us together at table, whatever the obstacles put in the way of the Spirit.

Introduction Endnotes

1. For some descriptions, see William Joseph Duschak, "Sunday Services Without the Priest," in Johannes Hofinger, ed., *Teaching All Nations: A Symposium on Modern Catechetics* (New York: Herder and Herder, 1961), 251–64; Johannes Hofinger, "Communal Worship in the Absence of a Priest: Its Importance and Structure," in Joseph Kellner, ed., *Worship, the Life of the Missions* (Notre Dame, IN: University of Notre Dame Press, 1958), 125–45; Jorge Kemerer, "A Priestless Sunday Service," *Worship* 37 (1963): 520–23.

2. Vatican II, *Decree on the Church's Missionary Activity (Ad gentes),* (December 7, 1965), no. 39. For the documents of Vatican II, I am using Norman P. Tanner, ed., *Decrees of the Ecumenical Councils* (Washington, D.C.: Georgetown University Press, 1990).

3. Ibid., no. 15.

4. See Monique Brulin, "Sunday Assemblies Without a Priest in France: Present Facts and Future Questions," *Concilium* 133 (1980): 29–36; Jan Kerkhofs, "Priests and 'Parishes' — A Statistical Survey," *Concilium* 133 (1980): 3–11. See also Centre National de Pastorale Liturgique, "Les laïcs dans la pastorale liturgique en France," *La Maison Dieu* 172 (1987): 107–15; Ferdinand Klostermann, *Gemeinde ohne Priester* (Mainz: Grünewald, 1981).

5. For French perspectives on the problem, see Jean Charles Didier, *Célébrer le Dimanche en l'Absence de Prêtre* (Chambray-lès Tours: C.L.D., 1984); Lucien Deiss, *Celebrations in the Absence of a Priest* (Phoenix: North American Liturgy Resources, 1989).

6. Dean Hoge, *The Future of Catholic Leadership — Responses to the Priest Shortage* (Kansas City: Sheed and Ward, 1987), 23–29.

7. Dennis Castillo, "The Origin of the Priest Shortage: 1942–1962," *America* 167 (24 October 1992): 302–304.

8. The results of their exhaustive study of the declining priest population may be found in *Full Pews and Empty Altars: Demographics of the Priest Shortage in United States Catholic Dioceses* (Madison, WI: University of Wisconsin Press, 1993).

9. See Bishops' Committee on the Liturgy, *Gathered in Steadfast Faith: Statement on Sunday Worship in the Absence of a Priest* [hereafter GSF] (Washington, D.C.: National Conference of Catholic Bishops, 1991). For a commentary, see John M. Huels, "Chronicle: Sunday Liturgies Without a Priest," *Worship* 64 (1990): 451–60.

10. See, for example, Donald Wuerl, "Thy Kingdom Come: New Beginnings in a Long Walk Together," *Origins* 18 (1988): 365–74; Rembert Weakland, "Future Parishes and the Priesthood Shortage," *Origins* 20 (1991): 535–40; Michael Sheehan, "Sunday Worship Without a Priest," *Origins* 21 (1992): 621–25.

11. Congregation for Divine Worship, *Directory for Sunday Celebrations in the Absence of a Priest*

[hereafter Directory] (June 2, 1988). The Directory may be found in *Origins* 18 (1988): 301 – 307. The cover letter (Prot. 691/ 86) with the Latin original, *Directorium de Celebrationibus Dominicalibus Absente Presbytero,* bore the date of May 30, 1988.

Earlier regulations are in the 1964 instruction from the Congregation of Rites, *Inter oecumenici,* no. 37, and in the 1983 *Codex Iuris Canonici,* Can. 1248,2. The instruction may be found in *Acta Apostolicae Sedis* 56 (1964): 884 – 85 and in *Documents on the Liturgy, 1963 – 1979: Conciliar, Papal, and Curial Texts* [hereafter DOL] (Collegeville: The Liturgical Press, 1982) [DOL 329].

12. Directory, no. 21.

13. GSF, no. 56.

14. "New changes spark controversy," *Gonzaga Bulletin* (November 8, 1984); "Bread or Stone?" *Credogram* 10, No. 1 (Fall 1988).

15. "What Are We SWAPing For?"

Communities Without the Eucharist

Throughout history, communities deprived of Sunday eucharist have been forced to find alternatives, either for the usual presiding minister at the eucharist or for the liturgy of the eucharist itself. Some of these communities have survived, have maintained their Christian identity and have continued in their mission. Others have not. To understand what can happen to a community that is prevented from celebrating the eucharist, we need to examine communities that have had to deal with eucharistic deprivation in the past. Since the issue is of importance beyond the Catholic communion, this chapter will include examples from other churches.

Alternative Ministries

Communities that have been separated from the larger church by persecution, isolation, doctrinal differences or other factors have rarely abandoned the tradition of a stable ministry whose members are authorized to preside at the eucharist in the name of the church. Normally, only ministers duly authorized—

usually by ordination—have been permitted to preside at a eucharist that the church as a whole would recognize. Thus, the various traditions emerging from the sixteenth-century Reformation have either maintained or reestablished pastoral ministries whose members preside at the eucharist, with the validity of these ministries accepted by churches in the same communion. Such ministers, however named, have effectively functioned in an episcopal or presbyteral role.

All rules, however, have exceptions. In at least two instances, churches have responded to a situation of possible eucharistic deprivation by providing substitutes for the usual presiders at the eucharist.

The Pre-Nicene Church.   Roman persecution was aimed at Christian worship rather than at Christian belief. The authorities, in trying to put an end to gatherings for worship, particularly sought out bishops, presbyters and other ministers. In the face of laws prohibiting meetings of secret societies, the fact that Christians continued to gather for worship shows how essential such gathering was to them—so much so that sometimes they would smuggle a presbyter and deacon *into* prison so that captives condemned to death could have the opportunity to celebrate the eucharist.[1]

Although it was the bishop who normally presided at the eucharist in the established communities of the second and third centuries, Ignatius of Antioch, writing in about 107 CE, had recognized that he could delegate the role: "Let that celebration of the eucharist be considered valid which is held under the bishop or anyone to whom he has committed it."[2] Presbyters were the likeliest candidates. In time, delegation of eucharistic presidency to presbyters was so customary that it became a part of their ordinary ministry.

Bishops also deputized substitute presiders for various other liturgical functions and apparently did not consider themselves always limited to choosing presbyters. Thus, Tertullian, writing in about 207 CE (while still Catholic) stated that the bishop may authorize presbyters and deacons to baptize and that in cases of urgent necessity, a lay man—but not a woman— might take it upon himself to baptize.[3] Hippolytus (c. 215 CE) allowed a presbyter or deacon to preside at the agape in the bishop's absence.[4] He also ranked confessors (those who had suffered for the faith) with presbyters.[5] Cyprian, bishop of Carthage from 248/249 to 258 CE, permitted a presbyter to reconcile penitents when he himself could not do so; he also allowed a deacon to reconcile if a presbyter was not available.[6]

As far as the eucharist is concerned, we have Tertullian's claim that a layman can preside in necessity. In an argument that laity are as bound as clergy to avoid digamy, he says:

> [W]here there is no such hierarchy, you yourself offer sacrifice, you baptize, and you are your own priest. Obviously, where there are three gathered together, even though they are lay persons, there is a church. . . . Therefore, if in time of necessity you have the right to exercise a priestly power, you must also need be living according to priestly discipline even when it is not necessary for you to exercise priestly powers."[7]

While Tertullian is not speaking of a stable or continuing alternative ministry, he does present his view that circumstances may require that someone other than the usual person provide priestly ministry.

By the time he wrote this (204–212), Tertullian was moving toward membership in the puritanical sect of Montanism, if he had not already shifted his allegiance. Because he was at odds with the broader church and its officials, his testimony might be suspect. Less open to question is the Synod of Arles (314), which implicitly recognized the legitimacy of an alternative ministry when it said: "Concerning deacons, whom we know to be offering in many places, it is our wish that this by no means be done."[8] The practice, apparently common, had probably originated during the Great Persecution under Diocletian (303–311). This extraordinary ministry was apparently regarded as unnecessary once the church was at peace. The wording of the canon, however, does not rule out the possibility that deacons might still need to preside in some circumstances and does not declare such celebrations invalid.

With peace for the church in the fourth century, eucharistic presidency was totally forbidden to deacons and laity. The understanding grew that bishops and presbyters were "priests" in a unique sense, even though all the faithful were a priestly people. As the title "priest" *(sacerdos)* came into common use, it included both presbyter and bishop. Presbyters were the ordinary presiders in outlying communities. When they celebrated with the bishop, though they did not participate in the same manner as the laity, they nevertheless functioned as members of the assembled community and were not concelebrants in the modern sense — i.e., "in the sense of consciously exercising in common some sort of sacramental 'power' proper to their order."[9] Yet it was at this time that the laity clearly became a distinct class and major liturgical roles were restricted to those in the "holy orders."[10]

In summary, it is evident that despite persecution, at least some pre-Nicene churches preserved themselves in a healthy state through flexibility regarding eucharistic presidency. At least some pre-Nicene bishops considered the eucharist too important to forego and consequently provided for substitute presiders in their absence, even if these had to be presbyters or nonpresbyters. However, these individuals apparently functioned with the (at least tacit) approval of the bishops and can be considered as having been, in effect, delegated by the bishop to preside at the eucharist. This presumably interacted in some way with their acceptance by other communities so that ecclesial communion was maintained, even without ordination. (In Chapter Five we will examine the relationship between the ordination of the presider and ecclesial communion.) In any case, the early church maintained itself by celebrating the Sunday eucharist, even if that meant providing substitutes for the usual presiders, because they realized that they could not live without it.

Contemporary Protestant Churches. A contemporary parallel to the situation and practice of the pre-Nicene church can be found in several Protestant traditions. The situation is generally that of isolated rural communities without pastors. The practice is either to delegate a layperson to preside or to ordain a presbyter whose ministry will be restricted to the local community. Both practices grow out of a renewed appreciation of the eucharist and the desire to celebrate it regularly, but with a conviction that the celebration is more important than the identity of the one who presides.

The Reformed church in France is one example of a modern church that has sought alternatives rather than forego the celebration of the eucharist.[11] Provision is made for a delegated layperson to preside at the Lord's Supper when a pastor is not available or when an emergency calls the pastor away. The delegate is generally someone who exercises a pastoral ministry in the community. For example, it may be a seminary student who is assigned to the community as an interim pastor. A presbyteral councillor (elder) of the local congregation is also a likely delegate in the pastor's absence. The delegation is temporary and is only for the particular place.

The Reformed church in France clearly recognizes the theological significance of pastoral ordination. Provision for delegation is based upon three premises: First, it is ultimately Christ who presides, whoever the delegated minister may be. Second, there is no "impassable gulf" between the priesthood of the baptized and the priesthood of pastors, although they are distinct. Third, presiding is a service to a community and is one that the community needs. The ultimate rationale is that it is more important that the community celebrate the Lord's Supper than that an ordained pastor preside at the celebration.

Some areas of the Episcopal church in South America have proposed that, in exceptional circumstances, lay leaders be licensed to preside at the eucharist. The proposal is that someone already involved in ministry, though not ready to make the lifelong commitment implied by ordination or not capable of broader priestly ministry, be suitably prepared, approved by the local community and licensed by the bishop to function in the community for a stated period.[12] The rationale is not only that communities would otherwise lack the eucharist; there is also the sense that communities celebrating the eucharist too infrequently would develop too high a theology of eucharist and ordination. Both the eucharist and the ordained presider could take on an almost magical aura if a special person, perhaps even one otherwise unknown to the community, were required for eucharistic celebration. The eucharist would thus be isolated from the community's daily life, coming from outside it and being almost foreign to it.[13]

However, the proposal for lay or delegated presidency was not accepted by the 1988 Lambeth Conference. The Anglican bishops preferred ordaining local people who could then preside at the eucharist or, as an alternative, having communion services using the reserved sacrament. Nevertheless, Anglicans have continued to discuss the advantages and disadvantages of occasional lay presidency at the eucharist.[14]

An alternative to lay or delegated presidency — especially in small, isolated or remote communities or in ethnically, linguistically or culturally distinct congregations that would otherwise lack sacramental and pastoral ministry — is the ordination of a "local" or "community" priest.[15] An individual who functions as a community leader is selected by the community, provided with training by the diocese, and ordained. Generally, the training is not in a seminary because it would be difficult, if not impossible, for the candidate to leave the community and family for an extended period. It is unlikely that the individual would ever function as a priest outside the community for which ordained; if "local" priests do move to another community, they are allowed to function only if the new congregation requests it and if the newly arrived "local priest" is licensed by the bishop. The pattern here is quite similar to that of the early church: Leadership emerges in the local community and is acknowledged by the broader church through "relative" ordination, that is, ordination for leadership in a particular community.[16]

The Evangelical Lutheran Church of America, on the other hand, has adopted a practice for small rural congregations unable to afford ordained leadership[17] that is similar to that found in the statement of the NCCB, *Gathered in Steadfast Faith*. At its August 1993 Assembly, it approved a new order of ministry — "diaconal ministers" — to lead such communities. In addition to other pastoral responsibilities, these ministers will preside at Sunday worship and minister communion from the reserved sacrament. An earlier practice, whereby bishops authorized deacons to preside at the eucharist, is apparently becoming less common.

Alternative Forms of Worship

Providing substitutes for the usual presiders, or otherwise changing the ordination discipline, has not been the characteristic response to a lack of clergy. The general practice has been to develop alternative forms of worship to substitute for the eucharist. However, almost all of the instances of this are from times when community celebration of the eucharist was not a priority; participation was minimal and lay liturgical roles were severely restricted even in ordinary circumstances because of strong clericalism. Because devotion was the primary expression of popular participation to begin with, a devotional service of some sort became the alternative to the eucharist.

Greenland. Christians — Irish monks — probably first came to Greenland in the late eighth and early ninth centuries. However, Christianity was not established as an organized church until Norse settlement in the early eleventh century. The first resident bishop seems to have arrived in 1126 and a diocese was established at Gardar in 1385. At the settlements' height in the twelfth and thirteenth centuries, the community was sizable: the Eastern Settlement had twelve churches, an Augustinian monastery and a Benedictine convent; the Western Settlement had four churches.

Because of climatic change, Eskimo attack, and Danish and Norwegian indifference due to the Black Death, the colony was lost and no bishop visited there after the beginning of the fifteenth century. The last dated connection between Greenland and the Nordic countries is about 1414.[18] In 1448, Pope Nicholas V wrote the bishops of Iceland, noting that Greenland had not had a resident bishop for thirty years and encouraging them to send priests and ordain a bishop for the Greenland church.[19] Though apparently no action was taken, absentee bishops continued to be named throughout the fifteenth century. In 1492, Pope Alexander VI appointed such a bishop and dispensed from the usual appointment fees in the hope that the new bishop would go to his diocese. The papal brief mentioned that no ship had visited Greenland in at least eighty years and claimed that "the inhabitants of that country have no recollection of the Christian faith."[20] Basing his comments on the pope's words, Archdale A. King says,

> The inhabitants had nothing left to remind them of the
> Christian religion, but a corporal which was exhibited
> once a year, upon which, one hundred years ago, the Body
> of Christ was consecrated by the last remaining priest
> there. . . . The inhabitants were thus lost to Christianity
> until the introduction of Lutheranism by the Danes in
> the 18th century.[21]

The pope's statement that the Christians of Greenland had
been without the eucharist for a century put the period in
round numbers, for two priests were still functioning in 1409,
one styling himself *officialis*. Alexander's unidentified oral
sources must themselves have been based on rumor and hearsay,
leading the pope to conclude that the people of Greenland
had reverted to paganism.[22] Unfortunately, we have too little
data either to be certain what state the church was in before
the colony disappeared or to be able to judge the accuracy
of the information available to Alexander VI.

Yet what the pope claims had substituted for the Mass seems
plausible. People were spectators in fifteenth-century liturgy, as
they had been for centuries. Allegorical interpretations of the
liturgy had attempted to make the most of this. If the people's
attention was not to be focused on communion at the table,
let them at least attend to a visual representation of the passion
in the ritual actions of the priest. From the early thirteenth
century, the elevation of the host enabled a visual communion
that was more consistent with this mode of participation than
was tactile communion, and it accordingly became what
Jungmann called "the pivot and center."[23] A devout look at the
corporal on which the host had rested was a likely liturgical
alternative. The veneration allegedly paid to the corporal suggests that the significance of the eucharist was vaguely remem-
bered but that devotion (or superstition) had substituted for
its celebration because there were no priests.

Only some monuments (including tombstones) and ruins
survive from the early Norse-Christian period.[24] No traces of
religious utensils have been found in the churches or in the
Eskimo settlements, suggesting that they had been removed
before the colonists died out. Yet, though no traces of European customs or Christian influence have been found among
the Eskimos,[25] for a time some graves continued to include

crosses, suggesting that customs outlived the faith. Without the eucharist, the church deteriorated. Whether it endured until the last colonists died is unknown.

Islamic Domination.   As the Mongols moved westward and as Islam spread, particularly with the rise of the Ottoman Turks, the ancient Oriental churches and the Orthodox churches of the East came under the control of non-Christians. Church activity was severely restricted. Nevertheless, Eastern Christians remained free to worship and to celebrate the Divine Liturgy. Orthodoxy *(orthodoxia* or *pravoslavie)* was primarily "true worship" or "proper praise," and the churches that bore that name managed to maintain themselves through little else. Though weakened, they did survive.

The situation was different for the Latin church. Hungary provides a specific example.[26] Turkish domination of half the country (from 1526 – 1731) led to as many as a third of the parishes being without priests. From about 1569, laypersons, particularly schoolmasters, were licensed to lead Sunday worship, baptize, witness marriages and provide other needed ministries. The practice continued in some parts of Hungary until at least 1748.

Why the Orthodox churches were able to continue worshiping under Islamic domination and the Latin church was not is unclear, nor is there detailed information available on how church life was affected. However, the Tridentine reform was only beginning at this time, so most people would have been accustomed to only infrequent communion. Devotional services, combined with catechesis and other forms of pastoral ministry, were sufficient for survival.

The *Kakure Kirishitan* of Japan.   The *kakure Kirishitan* ("hidden Christians") of Japan prove that Christian communities can survive without the eucharist for an extended period. However, the changes that took place over seven generations are examples of the risks that isolated communities face. Forms and practices survived, but often without their original Christian meanings.[27]

9

Francis Xavier made the first Japanese converts in 1548, and the first Catholic missionaries reached Japan in 1549. By the early seventeenth century, there were more than 400,000 Japanese Christians, with the diocese of Nagasaki the most important center. Renewed persecution, beginning with the expulsion of all missionaries in 1614, led to the suppression of Christianity and the loss of the Japanese church's contact with the outside world for more than two centuries.

The outside world first realized that vestiges of the church survived when Japanese sailors shipwrecked in the Philippines were found to have religious medals — regarded as charms — that had been passed down in their families.[28] The first renewed contact with the Japanese church came unexpectedly in 1865 in Nagasaki. About 30,000 to 35,000 hidden Christians had survived.

The original missionaries — always few in relation to the large numbers of baptized Christians but sympathetic to Japanese culture — had adapted themselves to the situation and organized the Japanese church in a way that enabled its survival. Converts were organized into sodalities or confraternities, small groups that met together for prayer, instruction and mutual support. The missionaries established a variety of lay ministries to preach and catechize, to baptize when a priest was not available and to care for the churches. Printed manuals were provided. Overall, preaching and devotional practices (especially the rosary and other religious articles) received more attention than did sacramental celebration. Since few of the converts had regular access to the sacraments, baptism was the only sacrament emphasized in catechesis.

Despite repeated persecutions, lack of clergy and the inability to celebrate the eucharist, small communities did manage to maintain themselves as identifiable groups in some continuity with sixteenth-century Catholicism. Most Christians who went underground had received little instruction and had not had much contact with the sacramental life of the church. Not surprisingly, changes took place. Catholic forms and practices were maintained even when their meaning was lost. Forms and practices closely resembling those of Japanese culture were the most likely to be retained, though they tended to be assimilated to folk Buddhism and Shinto.

10

The lay ministries established by the missionaries enabled the hidden Christians to develop their own system of religious leadership. The role and importance of these ministries varied in relation to the form of worship that was central in each of the different groups. Where the calendar was central, some officials were responsible for determining the dates for feastdays and for supervising the celebration of festivals. Where religious articles were the focus of worship, some officials were responsible for "closet gods" of various types, which were treated with a reverence like that earlier shown the eucharist. Officials were responsible for funerals and memorial services, for baptizing newborns, for assisting the dying and for leading prayer services. Corrupted Latin prayers and formulas were preserved, though their meaning was generally forgotten. Prayers translated into Japanese were more accurately preserved, though here, too, the meanings were often lost.

It is unclear whether the Christians who went underground did so without a clear distinction between Buddhism and Christianity or whether the two were assimilated to one another during the years spent in hiding. Shusaku Endo and others have claimed that the characteristic Japanese tolerance of the pantheistic mentality enabled Christianity to be planted and flourish, but that this same pantheistic mentality then transformed Christianity into a religious component of Japanese culture.[29] Little was available to Japanese Christians to help them maintain a distinctive Christian identity. Though the Bible had not been translated into Japanese before the persecutions, summaries of salvation history and Christian doctrine were passed on, with Buddhist terms and concepts and Japanese folklore mixed in.

There is no evidence that the lay leaders ever celebrated sacramental rites other than baptism; and the baptism of newborns did continue. However, nineteenth-century missionaries questioned the validity of these baptisms because the meaning of the formula — generally a mix of Japanese and broken Latin — was often practically lost. Sometimes the formula was spoken over water that the baby was given to drink! The notion of the eucharist as a sacrament to be received disappeared, although a corruption of the name survived.

In general, the hidden Christians maintained the devotionalism of sixteenth-century Catholicism. Various saints were honored and feastdays were kept. The rosary also survived, prayed corporately, changed in form and used with broken Latin prayers whose meanings were uncertain to the participants.

When Catholic missionaries returned to Japan in the second half of the nineteenth century, less than half of the hidden Christians were willing to enter communion with the Catholic church. Nineteenth-century missionaries had little sympathy for the "Japanization" of Christianity that had taken place over time and demanded a return to orthodoxy. But the hidden Christians saw this as a betrayal of their ancestors. Secrecy had become an important part of their religious life; they were unwilling to take the risk of becoming part of a public religious life.

About fifteen to twenty thousand descendants of the "Hidden Christians" currently survive. They remain secretive and refuse contact with the broader church. In effect, they have ceased to be part of the Christian church and instead practice a Japanese folk religion. But generally, even this is left behind as young people move to the cities. For most groups it is difficult now to find individuals willing to assume the leadership roles.

> In all probability, they will not survive long into the twenty-first century, if indeed they endure that long. They are an example of a largely unconscious blending of Christianity with traditional folk religion creating a new entity that by its very nature, village-bound and secret, prevents its continuance.[30]

There are similarities between the sixteenth-century missionary provisions and the practices advocated today for communities without regular eucharist: small, grass-roots support groups ("basic ecclesial communities"), lay ministers functioning as leaders and prayer services substituting for eucharistic celebration. However, there are also significant differences. The early Japanese converts were poorly instructed and never had regular access to the church's sacramental life. They went into hiding because of severe persecution. Cut off from communication with the broader church, they had no assistance in dealing with issues of cultural development and inculturation.

Nevertheless, the precedent suggests caution. These groups, isolated from the broader church and deprived of the eucharist, inculturated their Catholic faith, but much of that faith was lost. Though closely bonded to one another by their shared secret, they refused communion with the broader church.

The Russian "Priestless".[31]   In the seventeenth century, Patriarch Nikon of Moscow introduced liturgical reforms intended to bring the Russian Orthodox liturgy more in line with the Greek. Opponents, convinced that the "third Rome" had become heretical, like Rome and Constantinople, went into schism *(raskol)*. The *raskolniks* rejected the validity of Nikonian orders and, once their priests died, were priestless.

The Priestless, as they are called, organized themselves after a monastic pattern and were particularly strong in the north among villagers already unaccustomed to regular celebration of the Divine Liturgy. One group, the Shore Dwellers, came to hold that the church could exist without priesthood, with only two sacraments (baptism and penance) and with a fervent desire to share communion. Their liturgy included all services that could be conducted by laity. After an attempt at compulsory celibacy for all, they came to tolerate concubinage, abortion, child murder and illegitimacy. In time, they became more moderate and many returned to the Orthodox church. However, their doctrines influenced the Dukhobors and other mystical sects. The more radical of the Priestless formed such groups as the Theodosians (who continued to forbid marriage, leading to further breakups), the Philippians (very exclusive and severe, but in time more conventional), the Wanderers (highly individualistic pilgrims) and the Saviourites (who considered the period of the sacraments and public worship to be gone forever).

Eventually, most of the Priestless went from having two sacraments to having none at all, keeping only private prayers — unless they moved into religious indifferentism or Marxism. Beginning as religious fundamentalists, they ended in anarchism. Many returned to the Orthodox or to the Priestists (a group that had maintained priestly ministry and the Divine Liturgy). In the aftermath of the Bolshevik Revolution, the Priestless were practically exterminated.

American Methodism.   A major historical parallel with
the present situation of Catholic communities that cannot regularly participate in the eucharist is the situation of Methodists
in the United States. Methodism was originally a revival movement within the eighteenth-century Church of England. Trying to reach the unchurched multitudes, and in reaction to the
rationalism of the Enlightenment, "the people called Methodists" utilized lay preachers (including women) in their outreach.
Although alternative ministries (lay presiders at eucharist)
were sometimes used, an alternative to eucharist eventually
became standard, particularly on the American frontier.

John Wesley wanted his followers to share the Lord's Supper
at least weekly, if possible. Heart-oriented preaching services
supplemented the Anglican eucharist. When the eucharist was
not available, the love feast served as a substitute. Derivative
from the ancient *agape,* but using only bread and water, the love
feast was marked by spontaneity and a high level of participation; the sharing of prayer, testimony and hymn-singing enabled
the self-expression of the gathering.

The eucharistic emphasis of John Wesley and George
Whitefield led Robert Strawbridge and other North American
lay leaders in the 1760s to celebrate communion without
ordained elders.[32] The perceived necessity to do so came about
because the Anglican churches often refused to welcome
Methodists and because churches identified with England were
not attractive to revolution-minded colonists. Concluding
that, if they were called to preach, they were also called to
minister baptism and eucharist, in 1779 some ordained
themselves as well as others.

Opposition at the annual meeting and from Wesley himself
stopped this practice. The love feast, at which deacons or lay
preachers could preside, became more common than the
eucharist in the late eighteenth and early nineteenth century.
Ordained clergy were not provided until 1812. By then, a gen-
eration had grown accustomed to infrequent communion.
And in the fervor of the Second Great Awakening, the evange-
listic preaching service was more useful than the eucharist for
reaching the unchurched.

Black Methodist groups in the South had lost the eucharist
even earlier.[33] Local laws prevented blacks from holding positions

14

that required freedom of movement. As a result, black gatherings could celebrate the eucharist only with white elders. In addition, Southern black worship before Reconstruction centered on clandestine evening gatherings. Here, all could be involved in witness and in prayer that expressed true feelings, whereas the Sunday morning service required more circumspection.

The refusal of Anglican bishops to ordain ministers for the Methodist movement in the United States, in conjunction with social and cultural factors, led to the formation of a church largely led by lay preachers — though Wesley (not a bishop) himself ordained some ministers for the United States. The Americanization of the Wesleyan movement meant separation from the Episcopal church and internal dissension, particularly regarding ordination and the celebration of the other sacraments. Thus, for example, the Conference has sometimes authorized lay presiders for the eucharist. Although there is no laying on of hands, this is regarded as "temporary ordination."[34]

American Methodism achieved its success on the frontier, which did much to shape its character and polity — itinerant ministry (generally not ordained), camp meetings and revivals, emotional preaching, individualistic spontaneity and enthusiasm.[35] The Americanization of Protestant worship, through the frontier experience, showed itself particularly in "a pragmatic bent to do whatever is needed in worship and the freedom to do this uninhibited by canons or service books" in the effort to reach the unchurched.[36] Though camp meetings culminated in the celebration of baptism and the Lord's Supper, standard Sunday worship gave little place to the sacraments, centering instead on song, sermon and altar call.

The biblicism of frontier religion did give rise to a new denomination, the Christian Church (Disciples of Christ), which insisted on weekly eucharist because it had been practiced by the New Testament church.[37] Recognizing the charismatic character of New Testament ministry, the Disciples permitted a lay leadership at the eucharist that resonated with contemporary cultural trends, so that "Jacksonian democracy . . . reached even the eucharist in this radical form of liturgical equality."[38] In time, however, a professional, ordained clergy was instituted, apparently as the best way to maintain the order and decency in public worship that the New Testament called for.

American Methodism developed a strong social concern but lost the eucharistic emphasis of the Wesleys. Though the Lord's Supper was supposed to be celebrated quarterly if an ordained elder was available, a standard Sunday service that was centered on preaching developed. Architecturally, Methodist churches kept an altar surrounded by a communion rail, but the buildings were primarily for preaching and the rail (called the "altar") was more often used for declarations of personal conversion. By the early twentieth century, Wesley's eucharistic hymns had been dropped from the hymnal because the eucharist was largely lost and the eucharistic piety and fervor of the hymns seemed pointless. According to some reports, church attendance actually tended to decline when the Lord's Supper was celebrated, whether because of a sense of unworthiness on the part of church members or because of their unfamiliarity with the rite.

Hoyt Hickman remarks that Wesley's spiritual descendents are now comfortable with their lack of eucharist and adds:

> This may serve as a warning to others that a long continued practice of non-eucharistic Sunday worship may lead to a diminished desire for the eucharist, persisting even when there is no longer a shortage of clergy. Persistent eucharistic starvation shrinks the eucharistic appetite — a vicious spiral that, like anorexia, is not easily broken.[39]

For the most part, in the frontier tradition that has shaped many denominations in the United States, sacraments have been occasional visual aids to support the sermon. Television evangelists use the same basic worship pattern. The eucharist has receded into the background.

French Revolution. The French Revolution also made it necessary to develop alternative liturgies to the Sunday eucharist. The Civil Constitution of 1790, and the subsequently required oath to support it, divided the French church into a church loyal to Rome and a schismatic, constitutional church. Soon, because of the deportation, murder, emigration and execution of nonjuring priests — priests who refused to take the oath — Catholics loyal to Rome were effectively deprived of their clergy. During the Reign of Terror, juring clergy — those who had taken the oath — were also persecuted, and the

Constitutional church was itself destroyed. When freedom of worship was restored in 1794, dissension between jurors and nonjurors was rekindled. The return to power in 1797 of the more extreme revolutionary element led to renewed persecution and the deportation, execution or emigration of clergy.

Throughout this time, particularly in rural areas of France and Belgium, communities tried to maintain themselves even without clergy. In some parishes, priests were able to leave a consecrated host in the tabernacle or in a pyx to serve as a focus for communal worship. Parishes gathered for Sunday prayer — the reading of the Ordinary of the Mass (la messe blanche) or the recitation of the rosary — generally under the leadership of the schoolmaster. Not until Napoleon and Pius VII negotiated the Concordat of 1801 was a return to the eucharist possible.

It is difficult, if not impossible, to isolate the effect of the lack of the eucharist, particularly since it was only for a short period. The situation was complicated by persecution, a religious revival in reaction to the persecution and attitudinal shifts on the part of French Catholics. Moreover, eighteenth-century congregations, particularly in the country, had little involvement in the liturgy, though the situation had vastly improved over the seventeenth century.[40] Aside from realizing that their Sunday service was in the vernacular, it is likely that most communities hardly noticed the absence of the eucharist.

La Petite Église.   The schismatic "Little Church" provides a better example of a community long-deprived of eucharist. The Concordat of 1801, a compromise between the principles of the French Revolution and the prerevolutionary status of the church, repudiated the Civil Constitution of 1790, which had effectively put the French church into schism. In implementing the Concordat, Pius VII asked for the resignation of all bishops so that he could prepare the way for new appointments. Thirty-six bishops refused to resign and were supported by clergy (who were also required by the pope to resign their offices) and laity, leading to a schismatic "Little Church" in France and Belgium.

The schism went through three phases: It was first led by bishops without the pope (1801–1829), then by priests without bishops (1829–1847) and finally by laity without priests (1847–present). Although all the bishops eventually submitted, the last did not do so until 1829. By 1850, the communities that had opposed the Concordat no longer had priests and continued to decline in membership. In their gatherings they recited psalms, prayers and the rosary and were led by lay leaders, both men and women.[41]

The communities appealed to the First Vatican Council, but the Council was suspended before responding to them. Some contacts were made under Pope Pius XII. Three groups still existed in 1955.[42] Contact was again attempted under John XXIII and Paul VI, especially after the Second Vatican Council had recognized the sacramentality of the episcopate and the collegiality of bishops — two issues particularly important to the Little Church.[43]

The "Third World" Today. The situation and history of the church and its eucharist in the so-called "Third World" has not been studied a great deal. For that reason, comments on the character of this church, even in relation to the eucharist, are necessarily tentative and at risk of cultural bias. Still, the situation of the ordained ministry in the United States is not yet at the point it has reached in Latin America, for example, where there is now one priest for about every 5550 Catholics, with the ratio steadily worsening.[44]

The lack of priests and the consequent absence of the eucharist has affected various parts of Latin America, where Catholicism tends to be more devotional than sacramental and is particularly centered on the veneration of Mary and the saints. The Counter-Reformation piety of the early missionaries survives, closely intertwined with indigenous motifs. (Religious groups and/or movements such as *macumba* in Brazil, *santería* in Puerto Rico and Haiti and *curanderismo* in Mexico are, for the most part, syncretisms of Catholicism and pre-Columbian or African religions.) Typically, only the more well-to-do urban population has regular access to the eucharist.

Most North Americans interested in church renewal think of *comunidades de base* in connection with Latin America. The term is usually translated as "basic Christian communities" or "grassroots communities" but would be more accurately rendered "communities at the bottom." In context, it primarily refers to groups of the marginalized and oppressed poor who come together to empower themselves to seek liberation and the betterment of their situation. This new way of being church is the concrete expression of a liberation theology that regards the church, motivated by the gospel, as actively involved in transforming the world.[45] But because of their lack of authentic eucharistic experience, neither they nor the liberation theology that motivates them gives adequate attention to the role of the eucharist in the Christian community.

Popular religion — non-eucharistic and often regarded by foreign observers as syncretistic — does not necessarily provide a fertile ground for the growth of such faith communities.[46] The world of the poor, characterized by both piety and oppression, is also filled with demons and superhuman beings — and the poor are often more concerned with survival in such a world than with changing their condition. Insecurity is intensified when people are uprooted by urbanization. Thus, though popular religiosity is a rich resource of values and religious symbols, it is also regarded by some liberation theologians (such as Juan Luis Segundo) as an obstacle to liberation because its syncretistic and superstitious forms have often ended up legitimizing an oppressive system.

The situation may be largely the consequence of the inability of the poor to participate in the eucharist and to experience themselves as church in this context. Because of this inability, what takes place is not a cultural incarnation of Christianity whereby indigenous practices are transformed as they are assimilated. What results instead is a syncretism in which Christianity itself is transformed, as happened with the hidden Christians of Japan. (Leonardo Boff evaluates syncretism positively as the "Catholicity of Catholicism," but he seems to use the term as synonymous with acculturation rather than as it is generally used by comparative religionists.[47]) Without the eucharist, the poor are at the mercy of the cultural structuring of social relations, unimpeded by the concrete experience of the gospel in sacramental action. Admittedly, the eucharist has itself been in bondage, held captive by power structures and stereotypes of culture that have entered the church and its liturgy.[48] What is needed, then, is the liberation of the eucharist itself, something not possible while the church as a whole does not have access to it.

Due to a lack of priests, worship in the *comunidades de base* generally takes the form of a word service. Some liberation theologians, however (who have usually given little attention to the sacraments), propose that lay coordinators should preside at the community's celebration of the Lord's Supper.[49] Without the experience of eucharistic celebration among the poorer classes of Latin America, revitalization through *comunidades de base* generally leads to a sense of church centered more on word than on sacrament, congregational in orientation and with a deep social consciousness. An *iglesia popular* is distinguished from the broader church. Evangelical missionaries often receive a ready hearing.

The religious scene in Africa is even more diverse than that of Latin America. Unlike Islam, Christianity that was planted in African soil has produced a multitude of new religious movements. South of the Sahara, the African Independent Churches provide spiritual homes to between five and ten million people.[50] The churches include a wide range of Christian, semi-Christian and syncretistic groups, from the one-million strong Kimbanguist church to small local gatherings, with great differences in beliefs. A variety of economic, political, social and cultural factors has contributed to the origin of these groups, mostly over the last hundred years and generally connected with a yearning for a spiritually independent and truly African Christianity. Many of them still show their origin in traditional churches, including the Catholic church. Many of these groups lack the eucharist, perhaps an indication that they originated in communities unaccustomed to its celebration. In any case, beliefs show that the Africanization of Christianity has often fallen short of both continuity and communion.

Within the Catholic church itself it is necessary, as in Latin America, to distinguish between the "received" and the "lived" faith, since official religion and popular religiosity may be very different. In Benin, for example, the eucharist

> is perceived as the Bread of Heaven, and it is received as a mysterious remedy for the ills of existence. The holy fear it inspires, and that goes some way to explain why it

is expressly forbidden to receive communion in the hand, arises from the hidden forces the consecrated substance is thought to hide. Communion with the sacred Bread is essentially a participation in these mysterious forces rather than a making present once again of the paschal mystery, or a mystical union with Christ and his Body. The priest, through whom this mysterious transmutation of elements into Medications is effected, is in Benin thought of as being invested with redoubtable powers and forces.[51]

The quality of both the catechetical and the liturgical experience underlying these beliefs is questionable, and a logical connection to eucharistic deprivation is easily made.

Aylward Shorter, linking the Ethiopian and Sudanese famines of 1985, the Eucharistic Congress held that year and eucharistic famine, made a distinction between the church of the eucharistically privileged — which is able to celebrate the eucharist frequently — and the church of the eucharistically underprivileged — which cannot and instead marks Sunday with scripture, prayer and (occasionally) communion.[52] The latter, a majority, is increasing more rapidly than the increase in ordinations, with a ratio of one priest to 10,000 people in 1980.

Shorter presents the views of authors who consider the failure to provide presiders for the eucharist a grave infidelity to those who have a right to the eucharist. Priests necessarily become sacrament machines because a weak theology of priesthood considers the seminary education of clergy more significant than the community's right to the sacraments. People rarely celebrate the eucharist, even if they may occasionally have communion. Yet they are not fully aware that they are eucharistically undernourished — unfamiliar with the eucharist, not attracted to it or convinced of its value, because they cannot celebrate it in an African manner. Outside aid alone cannot solve the problem of famine until structures are transformed and people are able to feed themselves. Shorter presents this as an analogy for the eucharist:

> Ending the eucharistic famine in Africa demands new, local initiatives. The church has it in her power to end this famine. It is her duty to do so. But ending it demands boldness and originality and the readiness to modify recent, inessential traditions.[53]

Shorter's article focuses on the failure to inculturate marriage discipline and liturgy. As he indicates, Third World issues go far deeper than simply a lack of clergy and a consequent deprivation of eucharist. At their heart they concern the importation of European ecclesiology and liturgy and the failure to inculturate Christianity in diverse contexts. Simply providing more frequent communion services is not the solution.[54]

Conclusion

Except for American Methodism, Protestant Sunday worship has not been examined in this historical analysis. But something does need to be said about the eucharist in Protestantism. In many respects, the Reformation was a rediscovery of the eucharist, though subsequent history has been "a story of slow alternations of decline and revival."[55]

The sixteenth-century Protestant reformers on the continent — particularly Martin Luther and John Calvin — wanted to restore a community eucharist to Sunday worship but were unable to do so because the medieval heritage of congregational passivity meant that people were indifferent to the eucharist or willing to participate only on rare occasions. The reformers were thus forced to settle for a liturgy of the word because they refused to accept the "private Mass" at which only the priest received communion. Quarterly celebration of the eucharist became the standard Protestant pattern, and the word — rather than the sacrament — nourished faith and life. Later controversies between Anglicans and Puritans, along with the effects of the Enlightenment, further diminished sacramental consciousness.

Thus, eucharistic deprivation in the Protestant churches was not due to a lack of ordained presiders. The persistence of medieval attitudes preventing the restoration of the community eucharist and the rediscovery that the communion table — not the ritual actions of the priest — was to be central were strong factors. Still, it would be worthwhile to investigate the effects of the liturgical movement in Protestantism and the consequent restoration of the eucharist to prominence in some churches.[56]

How has the recovery of eucharistic celebration affected spirituality and the ecclesial sense of identity and mission?

Catholic and Protestant sixteenth-century reforms dealt differently with the medieval heritage of a clerical eucharist with little lay participation: Catholics maintained it while encouraging more frequent lay reception of communion, and Protestants rejected it while providing for an infrequent celebration of the eucharist with the hope of full lay participation on those occasions. The liturgical movement of the nineteenth and twentieth centuries has had a great deal of success in reversing this heritage, encouraging a return to the earlier tradition of Sunday eucharist celebrated by the assembled community. There is virtually no scientific data, however, concerning the effect this has had on the churches.

Our historical analysis shows that communities deprived of the Sunday eucharist have preferred to develop alternative forms of worship rather than provide substitutes for the usual presiders. Only in rare instances have churches made provision for someone other than the ordained priest to preside.

Worship alternatives have taken different forms. In an era when eucharistic experience itself was predominantly devotional, a devotional action or prayer service came to replace the celebration of the eucharist (Greenland, Hungary, French Revolution, *la Petite Église*). Where the eucharist had not been common, other forms of worship akin to those of indigenous religions have evolved as substitutes (Japan, parts of Latin America and Africa). More recently, because of influence from the biblical movement and Protestant traditions of worship, a liturgy centered on scripture has developed (in the *comunidades de base* of Latin America). In American Methodism, which provides the closest historical parallel to post-Vatican II Catholicism, a movement motivated by a tradition of eucharist has reverted to the standard post-Reformation Protestant liturgy centered on scripture. The *raskolniks* of Russian Orthodoxy, also from a eucharistic tradition, used monastic offices as the best substitute available for the Divine Liturgy.

Historical experience raises questions regarding the adequacy of such alternative liturgies. Admittedly, they have enabled communities to come together for worship on the Lord's Day and to express themselves as gatherings of the Body of Christ.

In situations where participation in the eucharist had not been prominent in popular religious life, they made it possible for communities to survive in a form that is still identifiable as Christian, at least in origin. But generally, they have meant that communities have either lost their taste for the eucharist (American Methodism) or have risked developing a highly clerical or even magical and otherworldly view of the church, the priesthood and the eucharist that is at odds with the tradition (the fears of South American Anglicans and a fact in parts of Africa).

Only further careful study can determine the extent to which the absence of community celebration of the eucharist has been responsible for mutations in the sense of ecclesial identity and mission in these communities. Still, the absence of the eucharist is associated with several negative developments: loss of membership, lack of interest in the broader church, uncritical acceptance of cultural influences, tendencies toward superstition and syncretism and, most alarmingly, a lack of interest in the eucharist itself. Historical experience supports the statement of the Second Vatican Council that "no Christian community can be built without roots and foundations in the celebration of the most holy eucharist."[57]

Obviously, examples from the past are not completely parallel to contemporary situations. Several of these communities suffered a total loss of the eucharist for an extended period, which is less likely to happen today. Most of the historical examples we have seen come from a time when the community's full participation in the eucharist was not appreciated. In an era when the eucharist was more devotion than community celebration, its replacement by a devotional service probably did not disrupt the community's spirituality or further diminish the ecclesial sense of identity and mission. But since the beginning of this century, we have been moving toward full, conscious and active participation of communities in the celebration of the eucharist. The extent to which this has been achieved will heighten the impact of not being able to celebrate the eucharist weekly.

But another practice advocated today may help restrain the negative effects. In Europe and the United States, Sunday worship in the absence of a priest has generally included an

element that, in the past, was rarely found in mission countries—
the reception of communion. Although the Catholic tradition
of reserving the eucharist after the celebration is longstanding,
lay eucharistic ministers are a recent innovation. Because of
this development, Sunday worship in the absence of a priest can
better parallel traditional Sunday worship by including both the
liturgy of the word and a service in which communion is
shared using bread already consecrated. If a devotional service
could substitute for the eucharist in an age when devotion was
the primary form of popular participation, can a communion
service do so today?

Chapter One
Endnotes

1. Gregory Dix, *The Shape of the Liturgy* (London: Dacre Press, 1945), 152.

2. *Letter to the Smyrnaeans,* 8, 1, in James A. Kleist, trans., *Ancient Christian Writers,* v. 1 (Westminster, MD: Newman Press, 1946), 93.

3. *De Baptismo,* 17. See André Hamman, ed., *Baptism: Ancient Liturgies and Patristic Texts* (Staten Island, NY: Alba House, 1967), 45. Later practice (e.g., in the *Apostolic Constitutions*) excluded deacons from this role except in emergencies, a discipline still upheld by the Orthodox churches.

4. *Apostolic Tradition,* 28. I've used the translation by G. J. Cuming, *Hippolytus: A Text for Students* (Bramcote: Grove, 1976), 25.

5. *Apostolic Tradition,* 9.

6. *Letter 18,* 1, 2. See G. W. Clarke, trans. and annot., *The Letters of St. Cyprian of Carthage,* v. 1, *Ancient Christian Writers,* v. 43 (New York: Newman Press, 1984), 98.

7. *De exhortatione castitatis,* 7, 2–6, in William P. Le Saint, trans., *Ancient Christian Writers,* v. 13 (New York: Newman Press, 1951), 53–54. Another, less explicit reference is in *De monogamia,* 12, 1–2 (pp. 98–100 in the same volume).

8. J.D. Mansi, ed., *Sacrorum Conciliorum Nova et Amplissima Collectio,* v. 2 (Paris: H. Welter, 1900–1927), 474.

9. Robert Taft, "*Ex Oriente Lux:* Some Reflections on Eucharistic Concelebration," in Kevin Seasoltz, ed., *Living Bread, Saving Cup: Readings on the Eucharist* (Collegeville: The Liturgical Press, 1987), 250. Taft notes that more is said about the roles of deacons and "laity" than about those of the presbyters.

10. See Alexandre Faivre, *The Emergence of the Laity in the Early Church* (New York: Paulist Press, 1990).

11. See Gaston Westphal, "Role and Limit of Pastoral Delegation to Laymen for the Celebration of the Eucharist in the Protestant Reformed Churches," in Matthew J. O'Connell, trans., *Roles in the Liturgical Assembly* (New York: Pueblo, 1981), 275–90.

12. Alan Hargrave, *But Who Will Preside?,* Grove Worship Series, No. 113 (Bramcote, Nottingham: Grove Books, 1990), 9–10.

13. Ibid., 5.

14. In addition to Hargrave, see Trevor Lloyd, ed., *Lay Presidency at the Eucharist?,* Grove Liturgical Study, No. 9 (Bramcote, Nottingham: Grove Books, 1977).

15. Title 3, Canon 9, *Constitutions and Canons for the Government of the Protestant Episcopal Church in the United States of America . . . Revised by the Convention 1991* [no further publication data]. I am grateful to Rev. Kristi Philip for her assistance in obtaining this information.

16. Karl Rahner, among other Catholics, has argued for a similar

practice for base communities; see his *The Shape of the Church to Come* (New York: Crossroad, 1974), 110. He explores this at greater length in "Pastoral Ministries and Community Leadership," *Theological Investigations,* v. 19 (New York: Crossroad, 1983), 73–86.

17. I am indebted to Dr. Robert Kugler for providing me with this information.

18. Finn Gad, *The History of Greenland,* vol. 1 (Montreal: McGill-Queen's University Press, 1971), 149.

19. Ibid., 157.

20. Ibid., 154.

21. Archdale A. King, *Liturgies of the Past* (London: Longmans, Green, 1959), 391.

22. Fin Gad, *The History of Greenland,* 180.

23. Joseph A. Jungmann, *The Mass of the Roman Rite: Its Origins and Development,* v. 2 (New York: Benziger, 1955), 208. The elevation of the chalice was not a common practice until prescribed in the Missal of Pius V. The risk of spilling, and the fact that the back part of the corporal was folded over the chalice, militated against doing so; the fact that the contents could not be seen anyway made it less significant.

24. Archdale A. King, *Liturgies of the Past,* 399.

25. Vilhjalmur Stefansson, *Unsolved Mysteries of the Artic* (New York: Macmillan, 1939), 13.

26. See Otto Nußbaum, *Sonntäglicher Gemeindegottesdienst ohne Priester: Liturgische und pastorale Überlegungen* (Wurzburg: Echter, 1985), 38. He cites one work (note 143, p. 38), which I have been unable to locate: K. Jubász, *Laien im Dienst der Seelsorge während der Türkenherrschaft in Ungarn* (Missionswissenschaftliche Abhandlungen und Texte 24 [1960]).

27. I am heavily indebted to Ann M. Harrington, *Japan's Hidden Christians* (Chicago: Loyola University Press, 1993). She provides a substantial bibliography (pages 191–197).

28. Otis Carey, *A History of Christianity in Japan* (Rutland, VT: C. E. Tuttle, 1976), 258.

29. Neil S. Fujita, *Japan's Encounter with Christianity: The Catholic Mission in Pre-Modern Japan* (New York: Paulist Press, 1991), 248.

30. Ann M. Harrington, *Japan's Hidden Christians,* 160.

31. Serge Bolshakoff, *Russian Nonconformity: The Story of "Unofficial" Religion in Russia* (Philadelphia: Westminster, 1950), 69–82. I am grateful to Dr. Stephen Happel of Catholic University for this reference.

32. Doug Adams, *Meeting House to Camp Meeting: Toward a History of American Free Church Worship from 1620 to 1835* (Sarasota: Modern Liturgy Resourse [sic] Publications, 1981), 103–104.

33. Ibid., 106–107.

34. Alan Hargrave, *But Who Will Preside?,* 16.

35. For the frontier tradition of worship, see James F. White, *Protestant Worship: Traditions in Transition* (Louisville, KY: Westminster/John Knox, 1989), 171–91.

36. James White, *Protestant Worship,* 172.

37. Doug Adams, *Meeting House to Camp Meeting,* 107–12; James White, *Protestant Worship,* 174–76.

38. James White, *Protestant Worship,* 175.

39. Hoyt L. Hickman, "Prayers of Thanksgiving in Non-Eucharistic Services," *Proceedings of the Annual Meeting of the North American Academy of Liturgy* (Nashville TN, 2–5 January 1989), 124.

40. Jean Delumeau, *Catholicism between Luther and Voltaire: A New View of the Counter-Reformation* (Philadelphia: Westminster Press, 1977), 197, 199.

41. E. Mangenot, "Anticoncordataires," *Dictionnaire de Théologie Catholique* (Paris: Letouzey et Ané, 1931), vol. 1/2, col. 1376.

42. *New Catholic Encyclopedia,* s.v. *"Petite Église,"* by L. P. Mahoney.

43. H. Maisonneuve, "Le drame de la 'Petite Église," *Melanges de Science Religieuse* 43 (1986): 177–99.

44. See René Laurentin, *Nouveaux ministères et fin du clergé* (Paris: 1971), 90–93, quoted by Leonardo Boff, *Ecclesiogenesis: The Base Communities Reinvent the Church* (Maryknoll, NY: Orbis, 1986), 61.

45. See, for example, Marcello deC. Azevedo, *Basic Ecclesial Communities in Brazil: The Challenge of a New Way of Being Church* (Washington, D.C.: Georgetown University Press, 1987).

46. For a study of varying evaluations of popular religion by liberation theologians and an attempt at a balanced synthesis, see Michael R. Candelaria, *Popular Religion and Liberation: The Dilemma of Liberation Theology* (Albany, NY: State University of New York Press, 1990). See also Enrique Dussel, "Popular Religion as Oppression and Liberation: Hypotheses on its Past and Present in Latin America," *Concilium* 186 (1986): 82–94.

47. See Leonardo Boff, *Church: Charism and Power: Liberation Theology and the Institutional Church* (New York: Crossroad, 1985), 89–107.

48. See Tissa Balasuriya, *The Eucharist and Human Liberation* (Maryknoll, NY: Orbis Books, 1977), 62. I have explored various aspects of this in "Liturgy and Justice for All," *Worship* 65 (1991): 290–306.

49. See, for example, Leonardo Boff, *Ecclesiogenesis,* 61–75. On the other hand, Karl Rahner, among others, argues that the community should be able to expect both legal recognition of its ecclesial status and "relative" ordination for its leader; see his *The Shape of the Church to Come,* 110–11 (above, note 16).

50. Harold Turner, "Independent Churches of African Origin and Form," *Concilium* 106 (1977): 105.

51. Sidbe Nemporé, "Popular Religion in Africa: Benin as a Typical Instance," *Concilium* 186 (1986): 47.

52. Aylward Shorter, "Eucharistic Famine in Africa," *African Ecclesiastical Review* 27 (1985): 131–37. He included in the latter group those who are temporarily or permanently excluded from communion by the church's marriage discipline.

53. Ibid., 136.

54. See also Herman J. Graf, "Priestless Sunday Services with Communion and Resulting Problems. A Report on an Ongoing Controversy," *East Asian Pastoral Review* 18 (1981): 175–89.

55. Yngve Brilioth, *Eucharistic Faith and Practice, Evangelical and Catholic* (London: S.P.C.K., 1930), 1.

56. For a survey of current practice, see Frank C. Senn, "The Frequency of Celebration and Reception of Communion in Protestantism," *Proceedings of the Annual Meeting of the North American Academy of Liturgy* (Saint Louis, Missouri, 2–5 January 1990), 98–118.

57. Vatican II, *Decree on the Ministry and Life of Priests (Presbyterorum ordinis),* (December 7, 1965), no. 6.

Sunday Worship
in the Absence of a Priest

The guidelines from both the Congregation for Divine Worship *(Directory for Sunday Celebrations in the Absence of a Priest)* and the U. S. Bishops' Committee on the Liturgy *(Gathered in Steadfast Faith)* recommend that members of those communities that are unable to celebrate the eucharist go elsewhere to join in its celebration, if that is possible.[1] If not, the members of the community should still maintain the sacramental significance of Sunday,[2] to the extent they can, by gathering for a Sunday celebration in the priest's absence in order to be nourished by the word, by common prayer and by sacramental communion, if possible.[3] The first recommendation — to go elsewhere for the eucharist — diminishes the local community and its witness to others and fails to appreciate the needs of those unable to travel. More significantly, it ignores the paramount role of the local faith community. The second option — Sunday worship in the absence of a priest (SWAP) — contains the recommendation to include a communion service if possible. While the communion service itself has been permitted for about 30 years now, it is a new dimension of SWAP. Can it prevent the erosion of community that has occurred in churches forced to find a replacement for the Sunday eucharist?

Of course, for many communities around the world the occurrence of a communion service is scarcely more frequent than a celebration of the eucharist itself. According to one informal survey, "in some communities the eucharist is celebrated once a month or once every two months; in other places, however, this occurs only once in six months or a year or even every two years."[4] In the same survey, the frequency of the communion service was found to vary almost as much because it is affected by the same factors that determine the frequency of the priest's visits.[5]

The recommended structure of SWAP closely parallels the structure of the traditional Sunday celebration of word and sacrament,[6] even though the documents warn against confusion with the eucharist and call for appropriate catechesis.[7] The source of confusion, however, is inherent in the structure of SWAP in that its liturgy of the word may be celebrated in the usual manner and its communion service consists of an act of thanksgiving and the usual communion rite. This leaves the impression that SWAP differs from Mass only in the absence of the priest and the institution narrative. Even beyond that, the communion service is especially problematic, particularly for people whose participation in the liturgy of the eucharist has largely been limited to receiving communion.

To maintain the distinction between the Mass and SWAP, *Gathered in Steadfast Faith* suggests Morning or Evening Prayer (with the scriptures of the day's Mass) as the first option for SWAP, and the liturgy of the word as the second option (18, 30, 53 – 54).[8] The *Directory* insists that the act of thanksgiving in the communion service is not to resemble the eucharistic prayer (45). *Gathered in Steadfast Faith,* which seems uncomfortable with the communion service, gives it less attention. Though it repeatedly mentions that communion may be distributed (6, 18, 30, 52) and states the significance of the communion service (28, 53, 54, 58),[9] it only once explicitly encourages communion outside of Mass (28) and once warns against the danger of separating communion from Mass (62). The impression is that the authors of the statement disagreed on the advisability of including the communion rite in SWAP.

The act of thanksgiving described in the *Directory* (45) risks becoming a eucharistic devotion. It may take place after the general intercessions or after communion, may be prayed while kneeling prior to the Lord's Prayer or after the sacrament has been placed on the altar, and "is directed to Christ in the eucharist." What often appears in SWAP is essentially a eucharistic prayer without the institution narrative. One recent publication of "priestless eucharistic services," for example, has a prayer of thanksgiving after communion but also a "prayer of community" before the communion rite. This "prayer of community" rather closely follows the structure and wording of the eucharistic prayers, but without the institution narrative.[10] Such practices leave the impression that SWAP with a communion rite is little different from the eucharist.

A communion service as a substitute for the eucharist is a recent innovation. While the tradition of reserving the eucharist is an old one, for centuries only ordained clergy have been permitted to serve as ministers of communion; a communion service with a lay leader was not an option. The development of a SWAP structure that includes a communion service seems to have begun in East Germany after World War II with the post-war displacement of millions of Catholics from Eastern Europe. Lay eucharistic ministers were apparently authorized on an experimental basis for one year in 1965, making it possible for the communion service to be added to the liturgy of the word. This authorization was extended for another three years in 1966 and permission was given for worldwide use of this ministry in 1967.[11] In the late 1960s and early 1970s, SWAP with a communion service was adopted in West Germany and Austria because of the large number of priestless parishes in those countries.[12] Other areas dealing with a declining number of priests soon did likewise. In the ten-year period between 1977 and 1987, the number of French communities regularly using SWAP increased nearly threefold.[13]

North American churches have had similar experiences. A 1987 national survey by the United States Bishops' Committee on the Liturgy showed that at least 40% of U.S. dioceses have parishes or missions administered by someone other than a priest. Nearly half of these dioceses had used SWAP in the previous year. Nearly one-third of all dioceses in the United States reported that parishes pastored by priests had used SWAP at least once during the previous year. Nearly 80% of the dioceses reported weekday celebrations of communion outside Mass in the absence of a priest, 17 dioceses had established guidelines for training leaders, 9 had a commissioning service and 20 had prepared orders of worship. About 80% of dioceses not presently using SWAP foresaw the need to do so in the future.[14] In response, many aids for training lay presiders have become available.[15]

While SWAP with a communion service is relatively new, the practice of sharing eucharistic communion apart from the celebration of the eucharist is not. An examination of the history of the practice will put us in a better position to evaluate whether SWAP with a communion service is an adequate substitute for the eucharist.

Communion Outside Mass

Historical antecedents to the modern communion service include various forms of communion outside Mass. From the earliest centuries we have examples of home communion and communion for the sick and dying. Somewhat later came the Liturgy of the Presanctified in the Eastern church, the Good Friday liturgy in the Western church and actual communion services, especially in medieval monasticism. In addition, the sharing of communion has sometimes been only loosely connected with the celebration of the eucharist, with communion ministered after, before and during Mass. Finally, the history of reserving the sacrament is itself a factor. Ideally, as with the cases of eucharistic deprivation noted in the first chapter, all of these should be correlated with the history of liturgical development, especially congregational participation in the eucharist, the medieval eucharistic controversies and eucharistic devotion, although this cannot be adequately done here.[16]

Communion for the Sick and Dying.   While the eucharist can be celebrated in the sickroom, the more convenient and more common practice through the centuries has been to bring communion from the eucharistic celebration or from the reserved sacrament to the sick person. In the mid-second century, Justin Martyr—the first to apply the term "eucharist" to the objects of bread and wine as well as to the action of celebration—concluded his description of the eucharistic action by stating, "the gifts over which the thanksgiving has been spoken [literally, "the thanksgivinged gifts"] are distributed, and everyone shares in them, while they are also sent via the deacons to the absent brethren."[17] Generally—again primarily for convenience—this has been done with the bread alone. While laity shared in this ministry in the early centuries, the Carolingian reformation reserved it exclusively to priests, a practice that remained with the church until recently.

Home Communion in the Early Centuries. Weekday celebration of the eucharist was an established practice no earlier than the late fourth century, and even then it was probably only among ascetics in northern Africa.[18] The practice was not common until the seventh century. Weekday communion, however, was more common and began earlier, although how widespread the practice was is occasionally questioned.[19] There is evidence of weekday communion at home in third-century Africa. In discouraging marriage to pagans, Tertullian mentions the difficulty of explaining the meaning of the eucharistic bread to a pagan spouse.[20] There is also evidence from Rome from the same period.[21] The practice of weekday communion at home seems to have continued in the fourth and fifth centuries. Basil, for example, says it was common practice among desert monks and Egyptian laity.[22]

The decline in the frequency of communion that began in the fourth century meant that domestic communion continued only among the pious. However common this domestic communion was, it should be emphasized that it was *domestic*—intended for a small household group or for individuals on weekdays in the interval between community celebrations of the eucharist. There is no evidence that it was ever used by a community on Sunday as a substitute for the celebration of the eucharist.

Liturgy of the Presanctified in the East.[23] The term is from the Greek *leitourgia tôn prohêgiasmenôn*. On weekdays when the Divine Liturgy — the eucharist — is not celebrated, the Byzantine rite has the tradition of a liturgy where the faithful, including the clergy, share bread sanctified at the previous celebration of the eucharist. The practice is especially common during Lent (on Wednesdays, on Fridays and on the first three days of Holy Week), when the older tradition of celebrating the Divine Liturgy only on Saturdays and Sundays is maintained.

At the liturgy where the eucharist is consecrated for a future occasion, this intended future use is emphasized in the ceremony by making a sign of the cross with the chalice over the bread to be reserved. When the Liturgy of the Presanctified is celebrated, communion is shared during the celebration of Vespers. The reserved bread is brought in procession to the altar, the Lord's Prayer is recited and the bread is presented to the people in the usual way but with the invitation, "Presanctified holy things for the holy." Then communion is shared. Some churches add other rites, including placing a particle of the bread in a chalice of unconsecrated wine — a "consecration by contact" also found in eighth-century France.

How this Liturgy of the Presanctified has functioned and been understood requires further investigation, for it is the only clear parallel to the form that SWAP is taking. However, it should be emphasized that this liturgy apparently took place *only on weekdays.* If, as is likely, it originated in the earlier domestic sharing of communion on weekdays, there would be an argument against its use by a community on Sunday.

Good Friday in the West.[24]   In the West, the Roman rite was unique in adopting the Liturgy of the Presanctified only for Good Friday, the only day when the eucharist may not be celebrated. Though the conservative Lateran did not do so, the parish churches of Rome began the practice in the seventh and eighth centuries, borrowing it from the East. The churches of northern Europe eventually followed a similar custom.

From the thirteenth century it was generally customary for the priest to share communion alone, apparently because no one else chose to do so. The custom became law in the 1570 Missal of Pius V. From the fourteenth century the procession to the repository and adoration at the repository became increasingly solemn. As in the East, the sanctified bread intended for a future communion service received special attention. Adoration of the reserved sacrament substituted for the people's communion, and the community liturgy became a eucharistic devotion.

Since the Holy Week reforms of 1955, all are once again able to share communion. Although the liturgy has varied over the centuries, the present rite is substantially the same as that of the past. The reserved bread is carried to the repository in solemn procession after the Holy Thursday liturgy. On Good Friday, communion is shared in the Office of the Passion (liturgy of the word and veneration of the cross). The ritual consists of bringing the reserved bread to the altar, praying the Lord's Prayer, and presenting and sharing communion in the usual way.

Communion Services.[25] Otto Nußbaum gives several instances of communion services, both connected with the Mass and completely separate from it, at which a priest, deacon or deaconess officiated.[26] In some cases as early as the ninth century, those not sharing communion were dismissed from Mass with the priest's blessing, and the communion service followed. Separate communion services, particularly in monasteries or convents without priests, easily developed. However, these appear to be exclusively weekday rather than Sunday celebrations and akin to the domestic communion services of the early centuries.

Since early monasteries rarely included priests in their membership, the monks usually participated in the local parish liturgy. Benedict's Rule, in fact, discouraged receiving priests as monks but did permit ordination of one or a few monks if it was necessary so that the monks could celebrate the eucharist. Priest-monks were few through at least the mid-seventh century, but that began to change in the eighth and ninth centuries. At first, the change was due to increased missionary and pastoral involvement. But later, clericalism — the prestige attached to the clerical state — had its effect, first in the ordination of monastic officials and then of other monks. At the same time, the understanding of the Mass was undergoing a major change. Each Mass came to be regarded as accomplishing something for God and for those offering it. More monks were therefore ordained and more Masses — usually private — were offered to the spiritual benefit of the monks and the stipend-givers, and to the financial benefit of the monasteries. Yet daily Mass was not widely recommended until the middle of the eighth century.[27] In general, the development of weekday Mass in both monastic and parochial settings was the consequence of the development of the liturgical cycle, not eucharistic devotion.[28]

But as late as the eleventh or early twelfth century, Monte Cassino and other monasteries had a liturgical service for sharing communion from the reserved sacrament. The service, called an *ordo*,[29] survives in at least four related manuscripts. Communities of women were even more dependent upon parishes or outside priests for the eucharist, although we apparently have only one manuscript with a communion service for women.

The Monte Cassino *ordo* is the more developed. Three psalms are chanted, followed by the *Kyrie,* the Lord's Prayer, and the Credo. Then there is a deprecatory absolution. Verses from the psalms and a series of prayers preparing for communion followed. Before communion was taken, the "Lord, I am not worthy" was prayed and a series of prayers "after communion" concluded the service. The formulas are in the singular and the masculine. A tenth- or eleventh-century manuscript, probably from France, gives a similar communion service, but all the formulas are feminine — some plural, some singular — and communion under both kinds is mentioned or supposed.

Characteristics of the services are significant. All relate communion to the eucharistic sacrifice. None copy the Mass, though several of the prayers before and after communion are from the Mass or develop themes found in similar prayers in the Mass. There is no liturgy of the word, understandable in communities that are celebrating the Liturgy of the Hours. Aspects of penitential and eucharistic devotions are combined: A sense of sin and culpability is prominent, along with the presence of an individualistic piety. The service incorporates "communion in the Body and Blood of the Lord into a celebration during the course of which the eucharistic mystery, such as it was conceived by the piety of the tenth and eleventh centuries, is evoked in all of its fullness."[30] In *The Rule of the*

Master, the leader ministered communion under both forms as the monks filed from None (mid-afternoon prayer) to the refectory, associating the eucharistic meal with the community table.[31]

What we have here is again something more akin to the weekday domestic communion of the early centuries than to the contemporary SWAP. At the stage of development where this was common, or where it continued in some religious communities in later centuries, the religious community, domestic in intent, was not considered a *eucharistic* community: Its members normally shared the Sunday eucharist with the rest of the local community. On weekdays, either because the local eucharistic community did not celebrate weekday eucharist or because participation in its celebration was inconvenient, the monastic community shared communion as households had done earlier. However, frequency of communion among monks and nuns also declined after the fourth century.

Communion After, Before and During Mass.[32] It was easy to move from a communion service at the end of Mass, after those not sharing were dismissed, to communion after Mass. Particularly when there were large crowds on communion days, it became common in the twelfth and thirteenth centuries for only the priest to receive during Mass and for the rest of the people to do so afterward. As communion became more frequent following the Council of Trent, some religious orders began the practice of communion outside Mass — even immediately after or before Mass — to make frequent communion easier. In 1905, when Pope Pius X encouraged frequent communion, the practice of communion outside Mass was further strengthened because it made frequent communion easier. On weekdays it was also quite common to give communion from the reserved sacrament before Mass for those who could not, or preferred not to, remain for the celebration. In large urban churches, communion was sometimes ministered continuously throughout the celebration, a practice explicitly permitted on Easter by the *Caeremoniale Episcoporum* of Clement VIII.[33]

These practices are clearly aberrations, concerned only with the convenience of individuals, whether communicants or priests. While they maintain a temporal connection with the liturgical celebration, they disengage individuals from that celebration and treat communion as primarily an individual devotion. Because these practices have existed on Sundays as well as on weekdays, they do provide a precedent for SWAP, but not an adequate one. SWAP looks to the needs of a community as well as to the needs of individuals, and SWAP is considered necessary only because the eucharist *cannot* be celebrated.

Reservation of the Eucharist.   All of the above-mentioned practices obviously assume that consecrated bread (and sometimes wine) is kept after the eucharistic celebration. Such reservation was first done for the sake of the sick and dying and then for any who might wish to receive communion. In an age when the approach to the eucharist was more devotional than actively participatory, it was easy for reservation to become a self-sufficient practice for the sake of venerating the eucharist and adoring Christ there present.

Though it is more difficult to understand, the practice of ministering communion from the reserved sacrament *during* Mass also came into being.[34] Unthinkable for a millennium — precisely because sharing the food from a previous celebration went against the meaning of the sacrifice metaphor — the practice began in the eleventh century.[35] In the context of the eucharistic controversies of that century, the conviction grew that Christ's real presence in the consecrated species was the important thing, not participation in the offering of the sacrifice. In time, as the eucharist as sacrament became distinct from the eucharist as sacrifice, the offering of the sacrifice became the priestly prerogative. The laity could only receive the sacrament and thereby participate in the sacrifice. Communion from the reserved sacrament was more practical, needing no consideration of the number of communicants. Frequency of communion increased after the Council of Trent, and communion from the reserved sacrament, once the exception, became the rule.

However, some commentators insisted that Trent preferred that people receive communion with bread consecrated at the Mass "so that the fruits of this sacrifice could be theirs more fully."[36] The Roman Missal spoke of consecrating enough bread for those receiving, for the sick and dying, and for those who might wish to receive communion outside Mass. It also mentioned a reserve in case the number of communicants was greater than expected. The ritual contained in the Roman Pontifical for the ordination of the subdeacon continued to contain the admonition to bring to the altar only as much bread as would be needed for those present.

Eighteenth-century controversy in Italy over the practice centered on communion at requiem Masses, but the resolution of the controversy by the Congregation of Rites in 1741 was clear: The eucharist should be received not simply *per modum sacramenti* (with preconsecrated hosts, as a means of sharing the eucharist as sacrament) but *per modum sacrificii* (with hosts consecrated at that Mass, as a means of sharing the eucharist as sacrifice). In 1742, Pope Benedict XIV, in the constitution *Certiores effecti* (addressed to the Italian bishops), stated that the preferred practice was for priest and people to share in the same offering. This was frequently emphasized in the course of the liturgical movement, and Pope Pius XII repeated Benedict XIV's statement in his encyclical on the liturgy, *Mediator Dei*.[37]

Vatican II "strongly encouraged that the people take part in the Mass more fully by receiving the body of the Lord, after the priest's communion, from the same sacrifice as that from which he has received."[38] The *General Instruction of the Roman Missal* is explicit:

> It is most desirable that the faithful receive the Lord's body from hosts consecrated at the same Mass and that, in the instances when it is permitted, they share in the chalice. Then even through the signs communion will stand out more clearly as a sharing in the sacrifice actually being celebrated.[39]

The document, *Holy Communion and Worship of the Eucharist outside Mass,* explains:

> Sacramental communion received during Mass is a more complete participation in the eucharistic celebration. This truth stands out more clearly, by force of the sign value, when after the priest's communion, the faithful receive the Lord's body and blood from the same sacrifice. Therefore, recently baked bread should ordinarily be consecrated in every eucharistic celebration for the communion of the faithful.[40]

This principle has been repeatedly emphasized since Vatican II, but contrary practices have not disappeared.

Post-conciliar documents by no means disapprove of reserving the eucharist, but they do place certain restrictions and conditions on the practice. The eucharist should not be reserved where Mass is celebrated, or at least not on the altar where Mass is celebrated.[41] The purpose of reservation is to unite Christ and the offering of his sacrifice with those otherwise not able to participate, especially the dying, the sick and the aged.[42]

Eucharistic devotion is by no means ruled out, but it must stay in close continuity with eucharistic celebration. This is necessary in order to maintain the dynamic character of the eucharist and not reduce it to an object that would function as sign of a static presence, a "being there" rather than a challenging invitation to the active relationship implied in taking, eating and drinking. It is also necessary to prevent the degeneration of eucharistic devotion into an individualistic piety lacking a scriptural foundation that would isolate the eucharist from both community and liturgy. As Vatican II said, "these devotions need to be kept under control . . . so that they cohere with the liturgy, in some way derive from it, and lead the people to it, inasmuch as the liturgy, by its nature, is far more important than they are."[43]

For that reason, postconciliar regulations regarding eucharistic reservation and devotion have strongly restricted previous practices. Current regulations are based on the principle that "the primary and original reason for reservation of the eucharist outside Mass is the administration of viaticum. The secondary ends are the giving of communion and the adoration of our Lord Jesus Christ present in the sacrament."[44] As a consequence, eucharistic reservation should not distract from the altar — the primary symbol of Christ for the celebrating community.[45] A separate eucharistic chapel is preferred.[46] Communion normally is not to be ministered apart from Mass.[47] Devotions should maintain the sense of Christ's active, ecclesial presence by deepening participation in the paschal mystery through clear relationship to the eucharistic sacrifice[48] and by a prayerful extension of the covenant into life through enabling people to deepen the union with Christ that takes place in communion.[49] Exposition of the sacrament is carefully regulated: Mass may not be celebrated during exposition,[50] exposition exclusively for the sake of giving benediction is prohibited,[51] and so-called perpetual adoration or exposition for an extended period of time is spoken of only in connection with religious communities who consider perpetual adoration to be part of their purpose.[52]

The efforts the postconciliar church has made to restrict and regulate — not eliminate — devotional practices suggest caution. Regular use of the communion service, especially on Sunday, runs the risk of perpetuating or restoring a devotional piety at odds with the dynamic of eucharistic celebration. Treating the eucharist as an object of devotion — almost unavoidable when the communion rite takes place outside of Mass — takes the eucharist out of its appropriate context, the action of community celebration.

Communion Service and Eucharist

A common value is apparent in every form of communion outside Mass, from the home communion of the second and third centuries to the SWAP of today. The value is participation in the eucharist when celebration *is not possible.* It is, in other words, an exception to the rule that the faithful gather to celebrate the eucharist. The risk of having the exception become the rule, both in ancient times and today, is that a changed perspective on the eucharist may develop. For example, Aidan Kavanagh has noted that the ascetics who received communion privately developed a concept of the eucharistic food as being primarily "medicine of the soul" rather than the publicly enacted sacrifice of redemption.[53] A corresponding risk in SWAP is that the communal celebration of a communion service will become a matter of individual communion devotions held in common — with the eucharist regarded as an object rather than as an action.

Does the communion service risk substituting eucharistic devotion for celebration? The history of communion outside Mass, with the exception of communion for the sick and dying, implies that possibility, perhaps even its inevitability. The history of Sunday worship shows that devotion has substituted for celebration even within the Mass. The *Directory* shows an awareness of this risk when it remarks that catechesis should emphasize that gathering even for the eucharist is a response to a call, not simply a matter of private devotion.[54]

Including a communion service within SWAP is particularly controversial among liturgists and sacramental theologians, even apart from the risk of perpetuating a devotional approach to the eucharist.[55] They call it a radical departure from the tradition of Sunday eucharist. They fear that, because the communion service gives SWAP a close resemblance to the eucharist, people may become satisfied with something less than the eucharist. They also question whether it is able, as participation in the eucharist is, to nurture and form participants in Catholic spirituality.

The Tradition of Sunday Eucharist.   Anything less than the full celebration of word and sacrament is certainly a departure from the constant Christian tradition. Both the *Directory* and *Gathered in Steadfast Faith* admit this in the emphasis they place on Sunday.[56] The close connection between the Lord's Day and the Lord's Supper is suggested in the New Testament and is clear in early witnesses. The tradition was maintained even during the centuries when few others apart from the priest were active participants in the celebration or shared in communion. Sunday and the eucharist, both sacraments of Christ's paschal mystery, imply one another and require one another for their full meaning. Robert Taft concludes that frequency of eucharistic celebration has varied over time, but "less than every Sunday can lay no claim to being traditional."[57]

The Christian Sunday, whatever the uncertainties of its origins and their possible association with anti-Judaism, is not simply the Jewish Sabbath transferred to another day.[58] First and foremost, Sunday is a sacrament of the risen Lord because it is the day of the resurrection, of Christ's appearances and of the Spirit's coming. Secondly and simultaneously, Sunday is the sacrament of the church because it is the day when the church is formed anew as the Body of Christ united with its Head. It is consequently a day of worship, of eucharistic worship; it is no day of rest, for like the disciples on the way to Emmaus, disciples know their Master as they come together, listen to God's Word and welcome one another at table. The

correlate of Christ's active, ecclesial presence in the action
of the eucharist is the active, responsive presence of his church
in that same action, not a passive reception. As the first day
of the week, Sunday is the day of creation, the day of light,
when God began to make a home for humanity. As the eighth
day, it is the day of the new creation, when God began to
make all things new. The Sunday celebration of the eucharist
anticipates its completion in God's eternal realm.

The close connection between Sunday and the eucharist
is assumed rather than argued in the New Testament and in
early Christian writings. The connection was made early and
is evident in several ways: in the regular association of Sunday
and the eucharist, in the development of a new and parallel
terminology, and in the interconnection of theological themes.

Sunday and the eucharist are regularly associated with each
other from very early on. In the New Testament, the characteristic beginning of the Jewish ritual meal — the breaking of
a loaf and the sharing of bread — has taken on a sufficiently
unique meaning that it can be used metonymously to identify
a prominent part of the life of the Christian community (Acts
2:42, 46). There is already a link between the first day, the
breaking of bread, the gathering of the community and the
responsibilities of disciples (Acts 10:41; 20:7, 11; 1 Corinthians
16:2). The *Didache* has the Christians gather for the breaking
of bread on the Lord's Day.[59] The pagan Pliny's reference to
"the appointed day" is likely Sunday.[60] Justin Martyr gives a
detailed account of the Sunday assembly for word and eucharist.[61] A century later the *Didaskalia* is explicit on the need
for the members of the Body of Christ to gather with their
Head on the Lord's Day to hear the word and be nourished
by the eucharist.[62]

Terminology also shows the connection between Sunday and
the eucharist. Revelation 1:10 speaks of "the Lord's day" *(he
kyriakē hēmera),* not "the day of the Lord" *(he hēmera tou kyriou),*
using the adjectival form to avoid confusion with the Old
Testament day of judgment. Paul uses the same adjectival con-
struction in 1 Corinthians 11:20 for "the Lord's supper" *(to
kyriakon deipnon).* The terminological parallel (Lord's day/Lord's
supper) was maintained beyond the New Testament era.

The same or similar theological themes are associated with both Sunday and the eucharist. The risen Lord's first-day appearances to his disciples (church-founding and mission-inaugurating appearances) are frequently in the context of meals, especially in Luke and John, and the eucharistic references are unmistakable. Second-century writers speak of the same themes in connection with both the Lord's day and the Lord's supper: creation, light, pasch, resurrection, fulfillment and anticipation of the eschaton.

In the course of the centuries, while weekday eucharist became customary, it was never on a par with the Sunday eucharist. Weekday eucharist nourishes personal devotion, but the Sunday eucharist is vital to the community's life and well-being. As Vatican II repeats, Sunday is the celebration of the Easter mystery, the fundamental feast day, the basis and center of the whole liturgical year and the day for sharing the eucharist.[63] The suggestion sometimes made that a community without a resident priest should gather when the priest is able to be with it, whatever the day of the week, thus misses the point of the sacramental significance of Sunday and the link between Sunday and the eucharist. It gives the priest greater importance than it gives to the gathering of the Body of Christ on the Lord's Day. This assembly is itself a celebration of the Easter mystery and is itself a sacrament of Christ. But the Sunday assembly is incomplete if it does not include the celebration of the Lord's Supper on the Lord's Day.

The origin of this tradition goes deeper than a chance association of the Lord's Day and the Lord's Supper. The New Testament accounts of the Last Supper, though they preserve different traditions, are alike (with the exception of John) in describing it as the institution of the eucharist in terms of a charge to the church. The formulation of the New Testament accounts shows the influence of liturgy, and it witnesses to the fact that the Lord's Supper — the breaking of bread — had already been a regular part of Christian worship before the scriptures were written.[64] The association originated from the Christian community's obedience to Jesus' command, "Do this in memory of me," and from the realization that the disciples of Jesus had communion with him in striving for his style of companionship at table, in affirming his death by their own self-offering and in giving themselves in service as he had.

There is a continuity between the inclusive meals of Jesus' ministry, the closed circle of the Last Supper and the missioning meals of the Risen Lord with his disciples. All these meals enact the companionship and communion found in God's kingdom. However, there is also discontinuity, and this discontinuity is crucial in appreciating the unique significance of the eucharist.

Jesus' message of God's unconditional love was prophetically enacted in inclusive or open-ended meals that scandalously violated religious standards by welcoming the outcast and the marginalized. People's refusal to accept this message led to Jesus' ultimate solidarity with the oppressed in his rejection and execution. This climactic sin establishes the first element of discontinuity. At the Last Supper, alienated from his people and in the closed company of his disciples, Jesus voluntarily identified himself with this fate — again through a parable-in-act or dramatized prophecy — and challenged his disciples to do likewise. The challenge was not simply to reconstitute the table companionship of Jesus' ministry; it was also the challenge to identify with Jesus' fate and the fate of the suffering and oppressed of the earth and, by doing so, to share in the new covenant that God was establishing in Jesus.

God's raising of Jesus from death establishes a second element of discontinuity. In the meals with the risen Lord, the closed circle opens as the disciples are filled with the Spirit and become church; they take on a new identity with Jesus and a new mission to the world.

While the eucharist, as the meal of the church and the sacrament of the church, derives in form from these meals, its meaning is from the whole of the Christ-event as summed up in the paschal mystery. As such, it does more than enact in continuity with these previous meals the companionship and communion of God's kingdom. Because it is marked by the discontinuities as well, it is the pre-eminent way of encountering the whole Christ, of sharing the new covenant with God grounded in Jesus' self-offering and of being transformed by the Spirit of the crucified and risen Lord into the Body of Christ called to service. The discontinuities also mean that the eucharist of the church is only open to those who put their faith in Jesus' saving death and who commit themselves to the work of building the Body that God raised from death.

The foci of later eucharistic theology were already clear in the eucharistic experience of the early church. They were all maintained to some extent in later theology, although medieval and post-Tridentine Catholic theology concentrated too much on Christ's presence and sacrifice. They are evident in contemporary ecumenical consensus. *Baptism, Eucharist and Ministry,* the Lima document of the Faith and Order Commission of the World Council of Churches, states the meaning of the eucharist in terms of liturgical experience: thanksgiving to the Father (3–4), anamnesis or memorial of Christ (5–13), invocation of the Spirit (14–18), the communion of the faithful (19–21) and the meal of the kingdom (22–26).[65]

These elements of meaning are unique to the eucharist and distinguish it from SWAP because the eucharist ritually enacts the paschal mystery of which each of these elements is an expression. Words enable mystery to be heard or overheard, and the rhetorical presentation of mystery persuades hearers to engage imagination and thought, to take positions and form intentions. Ritualizing goes beyond words — though it includes them — and *enacts* mystery in a bodily way so that it can be seen, tasted, smelled and touched. As a consequence, ritualizing is well adapted to forming and to transforming, both on the individual and corporate level — forming individuals into a community, and then transforming the community. This is because ritualizing is a matter of *doing* the mystery, not just talking about it.[66] (Jesus' command, after all, was to *do!*)

Though other ways of ritualizing the paschal mystery have been and continue to be invented, none have had the primal and enduring power that the eucharist has had through the centuries. Other rituals may hold more appeal for some individuals in some situations, but it is a matter of historical fact that no ritual has yet come close to dislodging the Lord's Supper from its central position. Its deep-seated association with the historical person of Jesus, with his death and resurrection and with the gathering of the Body of Christ through the centuries,[67] gives it an intrinsic meaning that no other ritual can assume.

Eucharist and Communion Service. For many people, SWAP may be simply a "priestless Mass." Despite official emphasis on the difference between the eucharist and SWAP, in practice the difference is blurred when parallel structures are maintained. This is the case with a liturgy of the word and communion service, especially when the service includes a prayer of thanksgiving hardly distinguishable from a eucharistic prayer except for the absence of the institution narrative. Laity who regard receiving communion as the essence of their participation in the eucharist are unlikely to feel deprived as long as consecrated hosts are available for SWAP. Will they also come to see the Mass as simply the means of providing those consecrated hosts?

There is a risk that people not only will be satisfied with SWAP, but will come to prefer it — though more for ecclesiological reasons than liturgical ones. J. Frank Henderson notes positive aspects "when lay people preside at Sunday worship":

> There is an emphasis on relatively small worshiping assemblies and often the relationship between the everyday life of the community and its worship is quite close. The necessary emphasis on the ministries of all the baptized is quite naturally accompanied by the establishment of a new relationship between priest and people. Team ministry, the sharing of ministries, and collective leadership, all provide models for new approaches to ministry in the church, both lay and ordained. The experience and creativity that are involved in the wide variety of ongoing training programs for lay ministers also may provide models for new approaches to the education of ordained ministers.[68]

Greater opportunities for participation are usually present with SWAP. Communities may put more time and energy into the preparation of SWAP than they do for the Mass, which is regarded as the priest's domain. The sense of shared responsibility often strengthens the sense of community. Generally, the lay presider is better known and more involved in the community's life than is the circuit-rider priest who visits only occasionally.

In some cases, the quality of celebration may even be better. Non-ordained worship leaders who are called to preside once a week can put more of themselves into their ministry than the priest who is called upon to preside four or more times on a weekend, as well as during the week. Yet Henderson's survey ten years ago concluded that the greatest liturgical problem associated with SWAP is the same as that associated with the Mass: poor celebration.[69]

Priestless parishes and SWAP with a communion service are both phenomena that have emerged too recently to have been studied as they need to be. Anecdotes abound, but careful sociological studies do not.[70] First of all, we need reliable data on the experience of communities using SWAP — particularly the experience of communities that have been using it for years — and then an analysis of this data to bring out its significance. We also need longitudinal studies, studies of particular communities over a period of time. If SWAP is indeed preferred, this is not only an indictment of the adequacy and quality of our eucharistic celebration; it is also an indication of the direction that needs to be taken in the ongoing catechetical and liturgical renewal in our communities.

Superficially, the ritual elements of the eucharist and of SWAP seem to be quite similar. In both, the action of eating together is central. In both, the gathered community first finds nourishment in God's word. In both, the table is set and thanks is given to God before sharing communion.

However, there are major differences. In the eucharist, the gifts that are presented are the work of human hands. In the communion service, they have been "presanctified," to use the Byzantine term. Though there is an act of thanksgiving in the communion service — which is itself a questionable practice because of the risk of confusion with the eucharistic prayer — the gifts are not "eucharistized" or "thanksgivinged" by that action. Instead, there is only an extrinsic relationship between this act of thanksgiving and the presanctified meal that will be shared. Because of the Catholic tradition of eucharistic reservation and eucharistic devotion, there will be a recurring temptation to make the thanksgiving an expression of gratitude for the sanctified meal, and perhaps even addressed to Christ. Similarly, the invocation of the Spirit is one-sided, directed only to the sanctification of the community, because the meal is already sanctified. After the presanctified bread has been put on the community's table, communion is more a union with Christ than a common union with Christ. Memorial tends to be a more individualistic and subjective calling to mind than a community action.

Everything hinges on the fact that the reserved sacrament, which was the object of one gathering's thanksgiving and will be the object of another gathering's dining, is, in the meantime, statically *there* and not caught up in the movement of the community's identification with Christ in the dynamics of companionship at table. The reserved sacrament is inevitably an object of devotion. When the sacrament is reserved, the movement from thanksgiving to dining is interrupted for the sake of those unable to be present, especially the dying. Eucharistic adoration is secondary, a by-product though certainly legitimate: During the hiatus, individuals may devote themselves to contemplating the sanctified gifts and thus stimulate their desire to enter more deeply into the community's actions of sacrifice and communion.

The dissonance is that thanksgiving and dining are dissociated because they are not the action of the same unique gathering. The particularity of the gathering characterizes each eucharist as the One Christ takes bread and cup, blesses God, and shares communion: What is new is the participation of the assembly. To the extent that the people, place and time are not the same in both actions, the ritual does not ring true and the gathering is not fully authentic.

Without a doubt, communion outside Mass, especially in Sunday community worship, is participation in the eucharist, a sharing in the sacramental celebration of the Easter mystery. But in the context of the communion service, eucharist is more a noun than a verb,[71] more an object than an action, and the community's participation is vicarious and mediated — either through its own previous celebration or the previous celebration of another community. The two experiences — Mass and the communion service — necessarily differ, even though superficially they seem to be the same. And if the sense of dissociation and dependency enters into the community's consciousness, the community will experience conflict.

Formation and Transformation

As SWAP becomes more common, what will be most evident immediately is a radical shift in communion practice. Until this century, Catholics had attended Mass without receiving communion. Although a gradual increase in the frequency of reception followed the Council of Trent, it was not until the twentieth century that the situation changed. Now the situation has begun to reverse, with many Catholics receiving communion without participating in Mass.

Many liturgists and sacramental theologians argue that it would be better if SWAP did not include a communion service. The discussion has been somewhat politicized: The impression is that proponents of the communion service want the situation to appear as normal as possible, and that opponents want to highlight what is missing in hopes of an outcry. Whether that impression is correct or not, the risks of the communion service must be kept in mind if the pastoral decision is made to provide for it. The issue will, however, remain purely theoretical for the majority of the world's Catholics, who have access to communion hardly more frequently than they have access to Mass.

Opponents of the communion service argue that appending it to the liturgy of the word implies that Christ is not present in the gathering of the community or in the word that is proclaimed and listened to in faith. They also fear that it will look like a Mass without a eucharistic prayer and will be confused with the Mass. They further claim, with some justification, that it will lead to a distorted understanding of the eucharist because it separates the sacrificial meal from the action of sacrifice. They perceive a distorted focus on the "real presence," the likelihood of an individualistic reception of communion, a misunderstanding of the eucharistic prayer as priestly consecration of bread and wine, and the mistaken belief that the laity's only action in the eucharist is the presentation of the gifts and the reception of communion.

Of course, these and other arguments can be countered, whether convincingly or not.[72] What is not as well answered is why there should be a communion service. Usually the answer is that people expect to be able to receive communion on

Sunday and without that possibility they will not attend—an indication of the political character of the discussion.

The weekday communion service has clear precedent in the tradition, all the way back to the home communion of the early centuries. There is no such precedent for the Sunday communion service, whose history goes back no further than the mid-1960s. The major issue is whether SWAP, even with eucharistic communion, is able to nurture and form participants in Catholic spirituality and shape a sense of ecclesial identity and mission. How long can the Body of Christ survive as such without the Lord's Supper on the Lord's Day? Official guidelines often gloss over this issue, although the U.S. guidelines seem more conscious than the *Directory* that SWAP, even with the communion service, will be a risk for the church.

Here again, concrete data and careful analysis are needed but are not yet available. What will emerge will probably be more a matter of degree than of radical difference. What will probably be most noticeable is a diminished ecclesial consciousness and a diminished sacramental consciousness—a movement in the direction of congregationalism and toward a church centered on the word without the sacrament. Why that is likely to be the case should become clearer in the next two chapters, as we first examine ecclesial communion and eucharistic celebration and then examine sacrifice and communion.

Chapter Two
Endnotes

1. Directory, no. 18; GSF, no. 18.

2. Directory, nos. 8–17; GSF, nos. 10–17. Both documents emphasize the role of the eucharist in doing so.

3. Directory, nos. 19–20, 32–33; GSF, nos. 5–6, 18, 28, 30. However, GSF regularly says that communion "may" be shared, it only once explicitly encourages it (28), and it warns of the danger of separating communion from the Mass (62).

4. J. Frank Henderson, "When Lay People Preside at Sunday Worship," *Worship* 58 (1984): 108.

5. Ibid., 112.

6. Especially in Directory; see nos. 35–50.

7. Directory, nos. 21–22; GSF, nos. 56–58.

8. Directory prefers the liturgy of the word, although it does mention the possibility of the liturgy of the hours (33).

9. The assembly unites itself to Christ's paschal mystery; receiving communion is sign, expression and accomplishment of union with those who are celebrating the eucharist.

10. Sydney Condray, *Assembled in Christ: 44 Liturgies with Lay Presiders* (Mystic, CT: Twenty-Third Publications, 1993).

11. C. Janssens, "Célébrations dominicales sans prêtre," *Questions Liturgiques* 2/3 (1983): 161.

12. William Marrevée, "'Priestless Masses'—At What Cost?" *Église et Théologie* 19 (1988): 208–209. (I am heavily indebted to Marrevée's excellent and stimulating article.) Because of the area of origin, most of the early literature is in German. For a discussion of the contemporary development and an extensive bibliography, see Nußbaum, *Sonntäglicher Gemeindegottesdienst ohne Priester,* especially pages 40–45.

13. See Monique Brulin, "Les assemblées dominicales en l'absence de prêtre, situation en France en 1987: Les résultats d'une enquéte nationale," *La Maison Dieu* 175 (1988): 111–67, especially 116, 121–22. For the 1977 survey, see Monique Brulin, "Assemblées dominicales en l'absence de prêtre, situation en France et enjeux pastoraux," *La Maison Dieu* 130 (1977): 80–113.

14. For a report on the consultation, see *BCL Newsletter* 24 (1988): 28–30.

15. Kathleen Hughes, *Lay Presiding: The Art of Leading Prayer* (Washington, D.C.: Pastoral Press, 1988); Center for Pastoral Liturgy, University of Notre Dame, *Leading the Community in Prayer: The Art of Presiding for Deacons and Lay Persons,* 76 minute video (Collegeville, MN: The Liturgical Press); Department of Communications, Diocese of Little Rock, *Ritual for Lay Presiders,* 27-minute video (Kansas City: Sheed and Ward); Institute for Pastoral Life, *Lay Presiders in Liturgy: The Experience and the Questions,* 90-minute video (Kansas City, MO: Sheed and Ward). *Assemblées dominicales en l'absence de prêtre* (Chambray-lès-

Tours: Centre National de Pastorale Liturgique, 1991) is a particularly valuable resource, as is the Western Liturgical Conference of Canada, *Ritual for Lay Presiders* (Regina, SK: Liturgy Commission, 1984).

16. See especially Nathan Mitchell, *Cult and Controversy: The Worship of the Eucharist Outside Mass* (New York: Liturgical Press/Pueblo, 1982); Miri Rubin, *Corpus Christi: The Eucharist in Late Medieval Culture* (Cambridge: Cambridge University Press, 1991).

17. *First Apology,* 1, 67. I have used the translation found in Lucien Deiss, ed., *Springtime of the Liturgy: Liturgical Texts of the First Four Centuries* (Collegeville: The Liturgical Press, 1979), 93–94.

18. Daniel Callam, "The Frequency of Mass in the Latin Church ca. 400," *Theological Studies* 45 (1984): 614.

19. Ibid., 615–16.

20. *Ad uxorem,* 2, 5. (*Ancient Christian Writers,* v. 13, p. 30). See also Tertullian, *De oratione,* 19; an English translation may be found in Ernest Evans, ed., *De oratione liber; Tract on Prayer* (London, SPCK, 1953).

21. In *De spectaculis,* 8, Novatian speaks of those who bring the eucharistic bread with them to the theater; see *Fathers of the Church,* v. 67 (Washington, DC: Catholic University of America Press, 1974). Hippolytus speaks of eating the eucharistic bread first and of keeping it safe from desecration (*Apostolic Tradition,* 36–37; Cuming, *Hippolytus,* 27).

22. *Letter 93.*

23. Otto Nußbaum, *Die Aufbewahrung der Eucharistie* (Bonn: Hanstein, 1979), 38–44.

24. See Bernard Capelle, "Le vendredi saint et la communion des fidèles," *Nouvelle Revue Théologique* 76 (1954): 142–154; Gerhard Römer, "Die Liturgie des Karfreitags," *Zeitschrift für katholischen Theologie* 77 (1955): 39–93, especially 86–93.

25. Jean Leclercq, "Eucharistic Celebrations Without Priests in the Middle Ages" in R. Kevin Seasoltz, ed., *Living Bread, Saving Cup: Readings on the Eucharist* (Collegeville: The Liturgical Press, 1987), 222–30. This was originally published in *Worship* 55 (1981): 160–68.

26. Otto Nußbaum, *Die Aufbewahrung der Eucharistie,* 44–50.

27. Cyrille Vogel, "Une mutation cultuelle inexpliquée: Le passage de l'Eucharistie communautaire à la messe privée," *Revue des Sciences Religieuses* 54 (1980): 237.

28. Robert Taft, "The Frequency of the Eucharist throughout History" in *Beyond East and West: Problems in Liturgical Understanding* (Washington, D.C.: Pastoral Press, 1984), 73.

29. It is significant that the service is called an *ordo* or "order." The term is traditionally used for the usual structure of an official liturgy ("order of Mass") or for a text that describes it *(ordines Romani).* Rome has insisted that the American ritual being prepared for use in SWAP *not* be called an "order."

30. Jean Leclercq, "Eucharistic Celebrations Without Priests," 229.

31. Gerard Austin, "Communion Services: A Break with Tradition?" in *Fountain of Life* (Washington, D.C.: Pastoral Press, 1991), 203–204.

32. Otto Nußbaum, *Die Aufbewahrung der Eucharistie,* 44–55.

33. *Caeremoniale Episcoporum,* II, c. 30; quoted by Peter Browe, "Wann fing man an, die Kommunion außerhalb der Messe auszuteilen?, *Theologie und Glaube* 23 (1931): 762n.

34. Otto Nußbaum, *Die Aufbewahrung der Eucharistie,* 55–61.

35. Peter Browe, *"Wann fing man an,"* 755. A sacrificial meal with food from a previous offering was impossible because it went against the basic meaning of sacrifice.

36. Council of Trent, "Teaching and Canons on the Most Holy Sacrifice of the Mass," Session 22, Chapter 6 (See Norman P. Tanner, ed., *Decrees of the Ecumenical Councils,* 734).

37. Pius XII, Encycl. *Mediator Dei* (November 20, 1947), no. 118.

38. Vatican II, *Constitution on the Liturgy (Sacrosanctum concilium)* [hereafter SC], (December 4, 1963), no. 55. (See Norman P. Tanner, *Decrees of the Ecumenical Councils,* 831.)

39. Congregation for Divine Worship, *General Instruction of the Roman Missal,* 4th ed. [hereafter GIRM], (March 27, 1975), no. 56h [DOL 208, no. 1446]. Later editions reference Congregation for the Discipline of the Sacraments, Instruction *Immensae caritatis* (January 29, 1973), no. 2 [DOL 264, nos. 2082–2084], as well as Congregation of Rites, Instruction *Eucharisticum mysterium* (May 25, 1967) nos. 31, 32 [DOL 179, nos. 1260, 1261].

40. Congregation for Divine Worship, *Holy Communion and Worship of the Eucharist outside Mass* [hereafter HCWEOM] (June 21, 1973), no. 13 [DOL 266, no. 2091].

41. HCWEOM, no.6 [DOL 279, no. 2198].

42. Congregation for Divine Worship, Decree *Eucharistiae sacramentum* (June 21, 1973) [DOL 265, no. 2089]; HCWEOM, no. 5 [DOL 279, no. 2097].

43. SC, no. 13.

44. HCWEOM, no. 5 [DOL 279, no. 2197].

45. HCWEOM, no. 6 [DOL 279, no. 2198].

46. HCWEOM, no. 9 [DOL 279, no. 2201].

47. HCWEOM, no. 14 [DOL 266, no. 2092].

48. HCWEOM, no. 80 [DOL 279, no. 2206].

49. HCWEOM, no. 81 [DOL 279, no. 2207].

50. HCWEOM, no. 83 [DOL 279, no. 2209].

51. HCWEOM, no. 89 [DOL 279, no. 2215]. The blessing must be preceded by a reasonable time

devoted to scripture readings, songs, prayers and silent prayer.

52. HCWEOM, no. 90 [DOL 279, no. 2216]. In other cases, it is only recommended that a lengthy exposition take place once a year.

53. Aidan Kavanagh, "Liturgy and Ecclesial Consciousness: A Dialectic of Change," *Studia Liturgica* 15 (1982/1983): 9.

54. Directory, no. 14.

55. On the Communion Service, in addition to Marrevée's article, "'Priestless Masses' — At What Cost?", see Gerard Austin, "Communion Services." The topic has also received attention in the popular press; e.g., Gabe Huck, "Why Settle for Communion? A Trend in the Wrong Direction," *Commonweal* (27 January 1989): 37 – 39; Tim Unsworth, "Catholics Won't Settle for Half a Mass," *U.S. Catholic* 54 (June 1989): 13 – 19. See also the report of the National Federation of Priests' Councils, "Priestless Parishes: Priests' Perspective," *Origins* 21 (1991): 50.

56. Directory, nos. 8 – 17; GSF, nos. 10 – 17.

57. Robert Taft, *Beyond East and West,* 74.

58. See, for example, Samuele Bacchiocchi, *From Sabbath to Sunday: A Historical Investigation of the Rise of Sunday Observance in Early Christianity* (Rome: Pontifical Gregorian University Press, 1977).

59. *Didache* 14. See also *Didache* 9 and 10. For an English translation see James A. Kleist trans., see *Ancient Christian Writers,* v. 1 (New York: Newman Press, 1948).

60. Letter 10 (to Trajan), 7. The letter was written about 112. The text may be found in Henry Bettenson, ed., *Documents of the Christian Church* (New York: Oxford University Press, 1963), 4.

61. *First Apology,* 67 (See Lucien Deiss, *Springtime of the Liturgy,* 93).

62. *Didaskalia,* 13 (See Lucien Deiss, *Springtime of the Liturgy,* 176 – 177).

63. SC, no. 106.

64. See, for example, Joachim Jeremias, *The Eucharistic Words of Jesus* (London: S.C.M. Press, 1966), 106 – 37.

65. Faith and Order Paper No. 111; World Council of Churches, 1982. For a study commissioned by the Catholic Theological Society of America, see Michael A. Fahey, ed., *Catholic Perspectives on Baptism, Eucharist, and Ministry* (Lanham, MD: University Press of America, 1986). The official Vatican response, from the Congregation of the Doctrine of the Faith, may be found in *Origins* 17 (1987): 401 – 16.

66. Ritual studies, although a new field, already has a vast amount of literature. For an introductory overview and bibliography, see *Liturgy Digest* 1 (Spring 1993).

67. For a lyrical description of how Jesus' command to "do this" has been obeyed "week by week and month by month, on a hundred thousand successive Sundays, faithfully, unfailingly, across all

the parishes of Christendom," see Gregory Dix, *The Shape of the Liturgy*, 744–45.

68. J. Frank Henderson, "When Lay People Preside," 116.

69. Ibid., 116–17.

70. One of the few presentations of data is that of Monique Brulin, "Les assemblées dominicales en l'absence de prêtre, situation française en 1987," cited above, note 13.

71. Gerard Austin, "Communion Services," 206.

72. For arguments and counterarguments, see Janssens, "Célébrations dominicales," 162–63; Reiner Kaczynski, "Sonntägliche Kommunionfeier: Irrweg order legitimer Ausweg?" in Alberich Martin Altermatt and Thaddäus A. Schnitker, eds., *Der Sonntag: Anspruch, Wirklichkeit, Gestalt* (Würzburg: Echter Verlag, 1986), 213–23.

Ecclesial Communion and Eucharistic Celebration

T he intimate relationship between Christ, the church and the eucharist is especially apparent in the recognition that the eucharist manifests the deepest reality of the church. "The eucharist makes the church"[1] on every level: parish community, local church and catholic church. It is, as Alexander Schmemann says, following Pseudo-Dionysius, "the sacrament of the assembly."[2] But the common union of communities in the eucharist is also a regional and worldwide bond because all eucharistic assemblies are united with God through Christ in the Spirit. Because of this, the church has consistently regulated who may share in the celebration, who may preside at the celebration and even who may be prayed for during the celebration. As the epiphany of the church, the eucharist and all that pertains to it is the expression of the church as a communion.

That the church is a communion — a sacramental communion of holy people and holy actions — has come again to our consciousness only in the nineteenth and twentieth centuries. In his 1943 encyclical, *Mystici corporis,* Pope Pius XII officially recognized the forgotten truth of the unity of Christians with Christ and with each other in a church that is both mystery and society.

In some respects, the never-discussed first chapter of the Schema *De Ecclesia* of the First Vatican Council prepared the way for this encyclical.[3] The understanding of the first chapter of *De Ecclesia* — that the church is a mystical body — echoed the nineteenth century revival of this theology by Johann Adam Möhler and Carlo Passaglia. While this first chapter was never discussed, written comments led to a revised draft that returned to Bellarmine's concept of church with its heavy emphasis on structure and institution. Had the Council completed its work, its teaching would probably have been along Bellarmine's lines and the revitalization of ecclesiology would have been delayed. The interruption of the Council prevented this from happening. The discarded first draft was utilized in Pope Leo XIII's encyclicals *Satis cognitum* (1896) and *Divinum illud* (1897), both of which in turn provided a foundation for *Mystici corporis.* While Leo stressed the structural and institutional elements of the church, his use of the earlier Vatican I draft gave official recognition to the fact that the church is more fundamentally *mystery,* the Body of Christ.

Theologians subsequently developed further the sacramental approach to the church.[4] The process of development culminated in Vatican II's extensively utilized concept of *communio,*[5] which is frequently described as the core of Vatican II's teaching on the church.[6] This, when applied to the church as the Body of Christ, maintains the conviction that Christ is continually founding the church to mirror his light, making it the "sacrament or instrumental sign of intimate union with God and of the unity of all humanity."[7] The church is being continually founded because, just as the church was part of what happened to Jesus in his resurrection as his Spirit poured out of the tomb, so it is maintained and renewed in his Spirit as it enters into the sacrament of his Easter mystery.

The church grows from this inner community with Christ, an inner community that is sacramentally expressed and effected in the eucharist. The universal church is a communion of churches sharing a common life: Christ. Each individual is united with Christ as assemblies identify with Christ by doing what he did. They need no external mediator; they need no mediator at all other than the Christ who is present to them in the Spirit, the Christ whose presence is sacramentally realized and celebrated in the church's life and worship. The Spirit mystically assimilates them to Christ, who in turn leads them to God. This Spirit, who flows to us from the paschal mystery, is actualized within us as we celebrate the eucharist. The eucharist is thus much more than a sacrament *in* the church — it is the sacrament *of* the church.

Sacramentality and a sacramental vision are therefore at the core of the church's identity.[8] In the West, the church of Rome and those churches closest to it have been foremost in maintaining the primacy of sacramentality and the consequent need to act sacramentally and thereby be sacrament. Believers — especially worshipers — are embodied. In their own embodiment and in all of creation, they recognize the mysterious presence of the divine. They feel the challenge to embody their faith and their worship in a life that will call attention to the incarnate presence of the divine.

This sacramental consciousness and vision is distinctively catholic (and Catholic). It is what has kept many people in the church. In fact, Andrew Greeley's study of the reasons people stay Catholic indicates that, more than any other factor, a personal conviction about the importance of the sacraments diminishes the likelihood of leaving the church by as much as half.[9] And when the quality of liturgical celebration is evaluated as excellent, the likelihood of staying in the church increases by another ten percentage points. The study offers sociological support for the theological and liturgical principles that the church makes the sacraments and the sacraments make the church. If that is the case, can we risk what the deprivation of the eucharist might mean to a community and to the church?

Church and Eucharist

Henri de Lubac has shown that the term "mystical body" originally referred to the eucharist and that the term "body of Christ" originally referred to the church.[10] However, as he shows, the patristic and early medieval recognition of the intimate and dynamic relationship between the church and the eucharist went deeper than this terminological parallel. The body of Christ raised from death, the mystical body of Christ in the eucharist, and the true body of Christ that is the church were understood as functions of one another. In time, attention narrowed to the relationship between the physical body of Christ and the eucharistic body of Christ, while the social and political implications of the community body were lost. The relationship between the church and the eucharist thus became tenuous.

1 Corinthians 11 contains the only New Testament commentaries on the eucharist and its celebration. In this letter, Paul points out to the Corinthians that their defective celebration of the Lord's Supper was, at its root, due to an erroneous sense of church, a failure to recognize the Body.[11] He contended that the divisions in the Corinthians' gathering showed that they did not come to eat the Lord's Supper (v. 20), that they despised the church (v. 22) or, at the least, failed to recognize the Body (v. 29) by not looking forward to one another's presence (v. 33). Earlier in the letter, Paul indicated that eucharistic communion implies and demands ecclesial community (10:16 – 17). In fact, his sense of the community as the Body of Christ may be the consequence of reflection on the many becoming one body through partaking of one loaf; for he begins with what is apparently a Christological concept of the Body of Christ (v. 16) and then moves through liturgical experience to an ecclesiological concept (v. 17).[12]

A later writer provides another example. Augustine encouraged the newly baptized to see their own mystery in the eucharist. He challenged them to recognize their own catechumenal journey of faith and transformation into the church not only in the dynamics of the celebration but even in the eucharistic bread. He emphasized that though the bread is consumed, its inner reality — the church — endures eternally.[13]

The Western church never completely lost sight of this. Despite the deficient liturgical celebrations of his day, Thomas Aquinas, for example, like Augustine before him, insisted that the unity of the church as Christ's mystical Body is the ultimate and enduring reality of the eucharist.[14] This was the consensus, if not the universal position, of scholastic theologians who, at least by the end of the twelfth century,[15] regarded the unified community-Body of Christ as the reality of the sacrament *(res sacramenti)* and the eucharistic presence ("real presence") as a symbolic reality *(res et sacramentum)* — a reality in its

62

own right but one that pointed beyond itself.[16] However, the medieval and Counter-Reformation preoccupation with the real presence did not go much beyond this symbolic reality *(res et sacramentum)* of the eucharistic presence. It stopped short of what Christ intended and failed to fully express the church's faith that the eucharist is oriented toward the unity and communion of Christ's mystical Body.

The liturgical reforms initiated by the Second Vatican Council have begun to provide a new experience of the church for Catholics, a new sense of church and mission that is the foundation for a new spirituality. Specific reforms make a new liturgical experience possible: scripture readings, common prayer and song are in the language of the people; several adult ministers share leadership in the celebration; the priest faces the people so that all stand together around the Lord's table. Not only is there a variety of options within the liturgy, there is also the possibility of further local adaptation. These and other liturgical changes make possible a new experience of church, one defined by common action and responsibility. Of course, it is not the liturgy as such but the full, active sharing as a community in the liturgy that is the source for imbibing the true Christian spirit.[17]

This new spirituality has by no means been fully achieved. Yet the direction in which we are moving is clear. The liturgy is celebrated by the assembly rather than by the priest. The liturgy is adapted to the local community rather than being universally identical. The liturgy emerges from human interaction and everyday life rather than being ritualistic and otherworldly. To the extent that any of this happens, the sense of church and mission changes. "Church" is more lay-centered and local than clerical and universal. It is actively involved in this world rather than simply concerned with providing a safe passage to another. It is global in character, concern and orientation. As all members of the community are called to participate in the liturgy, so all are called to be responsible for the church and its mission.

For most people, their primary experience of the church is the Sunday liturgy. In this new liturgical experience, the eucharist — the central act of the church — belongs to the people, who then begin to form the impression that the church and its mission are also theirs. Naturally enough, the new liturgical experience has led to the revival of the ancient eucharistic ecclesiology and to a new emphasis on the link between the eucharist and social justice.

Eucharistic Ecclesiology

The contemporary revival of eucharistic ecclesiology is primarily due to the patristic studies of the Russian Orthodox thinker Nikolaj Afanassiev (d. 1966). Eucharistic ecclesiology is based on the principle that the celebration of the eucharist presents a concrete ecclesiology. To know what the church is and does, look at what it is and what it does *when it gathers to celebrate the eucharist.*

Such an ecclesiology was never the sole ecclesiology in ancient times, nor can it be so today.[18] Nevertheless, eucharistic ecclesiology has proven its value: It provides a focus for ecumenical dialogue;[19] it is a dynamic ecclesiology that transcends the institutional view of church while providing a convincing rationale for ecclesiastical structures; its concreteness enables reflection on the church's mission and purpose to emerge from experience.

The Paschal Mystery. A eucharistic ecclesiology recognizes the paschal mystery as both the foundation of the church and as the church's fundamental constitution as sacramental communion of salvation. "Paschal mystery" is a concept prominent in patristic writings and ancient liturgies,[20] and it has come into prominence again in contemporary liturgical theology and in the teachings of Vatican II. It refers succinctly to our redemption and salvation through the death and resurrection of the Incarnate Word; it refers to our experience of redemption and salvation in the celebration of the sacraments. It is the basic paradigm of Christian spirituality.

"Mystery" is used here as in Ephesians 1:3 – 14: hidden in God, revealed in Christ, realized in us. The mystery is not a secret or a puzzle or an unintelligible reality. It is God revealed in, and to, human experience. It is, at its heart, God and

64

God's eternal plan of salvation as it touches human experience and transforms human history.

The mystery at work from eternity was revealed in history, especially in Christ. Its pattern became evident in the Passover of Israel and was accomplished in Christ, climaxing in his death and resurrection. Jesus, anointed by the Spirit in his incarnation and at his baptism, was crucified by sinful people and died. But God raised Jesus from death by the Spirit to be the risen glorified Lord, the firstborn of many children, who pours his Spirit on his disciples.

However, the mystery is not complete until it is realized in us through the outpouring of the Spirit. We experience its realization in the basic human sacraments of friendship and community. The outpouring of the Spirit is expressed and experienced liturgically in and through sacramental symbols, especially those of baptism and the eucharist. But the paschal mystery reaches beyond the liturgy to permeate all of Christian spirituality and to provide its most basic paradigm. As a consequence, the fundamental pattern of Christian living and Christian ethics is paschal: humanity moving in the Spirit, through Christ, to God.

The realization of the mystery was ritually anticipated at the Last Supper and is ritually memorialized in the Lord's Supper, where the disciples, like those going to Emmaus, know Christ's presence in their reaching out to others, their pondering human experience and their companionship with one another at table. In the celebration of the Lord's Supper, the activity of the community of disciples is twofold: They do the memorial of the Lord, and they know his presence as they do so. Those who enter into this twofold activity are those in whom the Spirit dwells. Christ thus perpetually originates his church when his disciples respond to his mandate.

The mystery of God saving us in Christ thus continues to be realized in us through our communion as church. The paschal mystery shapes the character of the church and directs its mission, aligning it with the work of God throughout creation and history. The process of initiation, climaxing in the communal celebration of baptism and the eucharist, brings us within this mystery and establishes our Christian identity. The regular celebration of the eucharist keeps us within this mystery and maintains our Christian identity. Baptism and the eucharist are thus the primary sacraments because they provide the most intense experience of the Crucified One who has been raised to life as Lord. The centrality of the paschal mystery thus establishes the fundamental importance of the eucharist for the identity and mission of the church.

The Communion of the Church.   Though eucharistic ecclesiology and an emphasis on the paschal mystery have been more characteristic of East than West, there is no doubt that the eucharist was a prominent starting point for ecclesiology in the early centuries in both East and West. "Church" was recognized as the local church, the community celebrating the eucharist with its bishop presiding. Two points are especially noticeable because of their contrast with the thought of later ages. First, "church" was primarily the concrete and tangible local church, the assembly gathered at a specific time and place and engaged in the common action of the eucharist. Second, the bishop's role as eucharistic leader and his role as pastoral leader correlated with one another. (Aspects of the first of these points will be considered in this section and in the one to follow. We will consider the correlation of liturgical and pastoral leadership in Chapter Five.)

The ecclesiology of the local church that is found in the teachings of the Second Vatican Council has a eucharistic ecclesiology as its starting point, even though this perspective is not easily reconcilable with the ecclesiological stance of the First Vatican Council. However, Vatican II takes a somewhat different direction than does the Russian Orthodox theology. Afanassiev contrasted his eucharistic ecclesiology with both Roman centralism and Orthodox synodalism by regarding "church" as the assembly united for the celebration of the eucharist. In Afanassiev's view, each community that celebrates the eucharist is completely church; unity with other communities is not constitutive of church. For the bishops of Vatican II, however, bonds of communion with other communities are part of the reality of being church. Thus, in the *Dogmatic Constitution on the Church* they say:

> [T]his church of Christ is truly present in all the *lawful* local congregations of the faithful which, *united to their*

shepherds, are themselves called churches in the New Testament" (emphasis added).[21]

"Local church" in normal Catholic usage thus refers to the diocesan church, the church in a given locality whose unity is symbolized by relationship to the bishop.

"Church" and "communion," because they are mystery, are not univocal terms. Although Vatican II speaks of the local church in diocesan terms (the community pastored by a bishop), it does not develop a complete theology of the local church. There are grounds for arguing that the community pastored by the bishop's delegate is also local church.[22] Increasingly, the terms "church" and "communion" are being applied "from the bottom up." Thus, for Leonardo Boff, since faith is given essentially as communion,

> believers, by reason of their faith-and-community, are already, in themselves, the presence of the universal church, with this becoming more visible when they gather with a leader who is symbol of their unity with one another and other such communities.[23]

The eucharistic assembly is, correspondingly, more readily and intensely experienced as church, and Vatican II does speak of it in such terms when it states that there is a close connection between eucharist and church.[24] In every such community, however small or poor or isolated, "Christ is present and the power of his presence gathers together the one, holy, catholic, and apostolic church."[25]

The fact is that "church" and "communion" do not have a single referent. Church and communion, as human realizations of the paschal mystery, exist simultaneously on different levels. But they always have a common center — Christ — who is immediately present in the Spirit to the faithful. For that reason, on every level the unity is an inward unity and ecclesial communion is a mutual interiority because it is a common union with Christ.

As a mystery of communion, "church," as used in the New Testament, likewise transcends the precision of a single referent. New Testament usage, particularly in the writings of Paul, started with the experience of the house church. But with growth, particularly in larger cities, it was necessary to coordinate, unify and even centralize the various house churches that existed in an area. It was also necessary that the several house churches mutually recognize each other in one church. (Early insistence on unity, harmony and hospitality suggests that efforts were already being made to deal with tension and even rivalry.) This mutual recognition in Christ came to be symbolized by the relationship of the house churches to the bishop, perhaps to compensate for the fact that this broader meaning of church was necessarily more abstract and in need of a concrete, visible expression.

For ease of communication it may be best to reserve the terms "local church" and "particular church" for the diocesan church, at least until the theology of local church is more adequately developed. But it is necessary to recognize that the diocesan church is itself the communion of many eucharistic and faith communities, which are themselves the realization of church in a more limited but still inclusive communion. Beyond that, on every level, it is through the eucharist that communion is expressed and maintained. This is accomplished not only verbally but also primarily in the Spirit through the common center, Christ, and symbolically through the priest, the bishop's delegate. "The cup of blessing that we bless, is it not a sharing in the blood of Christ? The bread that we break, is it not a sharing in the body of Christ? Because there is one bread, we who are many are one body, for we all partake of the one bread" (1 Corinthians 10:16–17). The risk, then, is that infrequent Sunday eucharist will weaken communion — *on every level.* It is not merely the communion of the parish without the eucharist that suffers. Because ecclesial communion is an inward unity, a mutual interiority, "if one member suffers, all suffer together with it" (1 Corinthians 12:26).

In any case, the *Dogmatic Constitution on the Church* sets the legal and the ministerial side by side when it maintains that ecclesial reality correlates with ecclesial communion. This does not mean that the reality and legitimacy of the local church depend simply upon external legal recognition. The local church's communion with its pastors is an internal reality, communion with the broader church is an internal reality, and communion in the Holy Spirit is an internal reality. Ecclesial communion is thus an inward unity, not something derived from outside. Even the Petrine ministry, charged to maintain unity and communion, is interior to the local church.[26] Ecclesial communion is a coincidence of communities in Christ, their common center, rather than an external linking: "In and from these particular churches there exists the one unique catholic church."[27]

As a consequence, the local church is indeed self-responsible. Its ecclesial character is a gift in the Spirit and not something received from an outside source. As a result, its primary responsibility is to the Spirit that dwells within it and from which it draws its life in Christ. But this self-responsibility does not mean that it is isolated and self-sufficient. The same Spirit indwells other communities and is thus a common source of unity and life. For that reason, a local or particular church — or a eucharistic community — that seeks self-sufficiency also weakens communion because it fails to draw its life from the Spirit. This is true whether a local church seeks self-sufficiency by acting apart from the communion or by trying to dominate and control other local churches.

The Sacramental Character of the Local Church.

The communion or common union of the local church is sacramental on several levels because it is the coincidence of communities in Christ. It is sacramental because *this* church is *the* church in this place. It is sacramental because the signs and symbols of communion (including the external ones, as we will see, of bishop and priest) manifest the presence of the Spirit of Christ. It is sacramental because it expresses and effects the communion of the universal church in the one Christ who is inwardly present to the local church in the Spirit. It is sacramental because it manifests the communion of saints.

The sacramental character of the communion of the local church shows that the church is itself an act of communion effected by God. Because the church is the human realization of the paschal mystery and an act of communion that images the Triune God, the church is sacrament: As the dwelling place of God it is transformed to manifest the mysterious, incarnate presence of the Divine. It acts sacramentally to transform the world, especially by working for justice. But above all, the church is an act of communion because it is *acting:* It is doing what Jesus the host and servant did, is being identified with him, and is thus being transformed by the paschal mystery.

69

The basic structure of the church, then, is eucharistic, and the eucharist is the "root and center of ecclesial communion."[28] In the celebration of the eucharist, the local church manifests its communion as the Body of Christ and shows that the source of its unity is God-in-Christ. This communion is not merely with those who are then and there celebrating the eucharist, nor is the local church in communion only with those who are now living: It is part of the communion of saints, that eschatological reality that grows into the reign of God. As the ritual meal by which the Body of Christ is nourished and strengthened, the eucharist is the center of the communion of saints. Because the common center is the risen Christ, the *communio sanctorum* is a communion of saints who have through the centuries shared in the holy action that makes them holy by including them in the Paschal Mystery.

Within this perspective, the ministry of eucharistic presidency is itself sacramental of ecclesial communion and not the exercise of an exclusive power. The bishop presides in the *agape* and at the eucharist because he is the community's pastoral leader, its leader in the everyday life of love. As such, the bishop functions as a sign of communion and a sign of Christ. The collegiality of bishops (formulated at Vatican II to balance Vatican I's emphasis on the Petrine primacy) is more accurately a communion, for each bishop is not merely part of a whole that requires Peter for completeness — an impression given by the term "college" — no more than the relationship of local church and universal church is one of part to whole.[29] Rather, as Cyprian says, there is only "one episcopacy"[30] and "one chair, founded by the Lord's authority, upon Peter";[31] thus, each bishop is the expression and representation of the whole, and the Petrine ministry is exercised within the local church. This same sacramental understanding underlies Ignatius of Antioch's emphasis on an authentic eucharist being one at which the bishop or the bishop's delegate presided:[32] The bishop's presence in the delegate expressed and represented the communion with the whole church that is manifested in the eucharistic assembly.

The Character of the Eucharist. If eucharistic ecclesiology is to be more than a decorative veneer or more than a canonization of cultural trends, the character of the eucharist must be recognized from its origins. These origins include Jesus' meals during his ministry, his Last Supper with his disciples and the early church's recognition of its table-companionship as being a communion with the risen Lord. There is a continuity in form among these three points of origin, even if meaning varies among them. Both the continuities and the discontinuities enter into the character of the eucharist.

Jesus' meals during his ministry show that the eucharist is the ever-expanding and all-inclusive life-center of the entire Christian community. Jesus made a point of being at table with those who fell short of religious standards. In so doing, he provided a prophetic sign of God's intentions, dramatizing God's unconditional love and modeling God's will. The inclusive quality of Jesus' meals requires that all members of the assembly recognize their responsibility to welcome one another; limits to hospitality are to be as restricted as possible. The inclusive quality of Jesus' meals also means that the gap between the eucharistically overprivileged and the eucharistically underprivileged cannot be allowed to stand.

The tradition represented by John and the *Didache* looks to Jesus' hosting the crowds, rather than to the Last Supper, as the institution of the church's eucharist. (However, the resurrection motif is strong in John 6:51b – 58.) This, as well as Jesus' parable on the meaning of community (Luke 10:29 – 37), challenges views of liturgical community that would otherwise regard it as a small gathering of intimates, familial or otherwise. Rather than being simply the *expression* of community, the eucharist is more fundamentally the challenge and the power to *become* an ever more inclusive community. As a consequence, communities deprived of the eucharist are deprived of the strongest sacrament of their source of life.

In every gospel tradition, the Last Supper is the occasion when Jesus forms the community of his disciples into his living memorial. In the synoptic and Pauline traditions, Jesus commissions his disciples to continue his ministry of companionship at table. By making their meals together like his Supper, their meals *are* his Supper and they experience him anew. In the Johannine tradition, the charge that Jesus gave to the church at the Last Supper was to memorialize him, not through table rituals but through concrete service. After washing their feet,

Jesus challenged his disciples to memorialize him as servant by washing one another's feet. And in so doing, the disciples are no longer servants, but friends!

Eucharist must lead to mission. Hospitality at table must extend to the most minute details of daily life — and to death — or else the meal will be merely a superficial camaraderie. Yet the Johannine tradition can itself be challenged: Service without the friendship of the shared table will be no more than a professional-client relationship. The inversion of social relationships that characterizes Christianity is for the sake of encouraging a radical equality and an unconditional willingness among believers to accept one another. This is manifested when disciples host one another at table and serve one another's needs. The intimacy of eucharistic communion contains the force that turns disciples into servants — sharers of themselves — even unto death. In proclaiming the Lord's death until he comes again, disciples commit themselves to building up the Lord's Body.

The frequency with which the post-Easter appearances are in the context of meal-sharing gives a final indication of the eucharist's importance for the ecclesial reality of communities. The appearances of the risen Christ establish the community of disciples as the Body of Christ — the church — and associate it with the mission of Christ in the Spirit. The meals of the ministry, transformed at the Last Supper, are again transformed as continuing communion with Christ is experienced in post-Easter meals. Communities must celebrate the eucharist so that they will be church and will share both its communion and its mission.

All of the meals that the disciples shared with Jesus were Jesus' attempts to share with them his experience of God's reign, humanly manifested in what we have come to call the communion of saints. The Last Supper, at least in retrospect, was the penultimate step of the disciples toward Easter faith. But it was at Easter that the Spirit of God gathered the disciples together. It was then that they once more heard his voice and knew him as the Word of God. As they tried to make their table-companionship like his, they knew him in the sharing of the bread and of the cup of blessing, and they knew themselves as his Body. Made into his Body, they then went out to continue his work of service.

Despite the frequency with which the risen Lord arrives at mealtime in the resurrection narratives, emphasizing that the resurrection appearances are more concerned with establishing the eschatological community undermines a devotional approach to the eucharist that would see it as a way for Jesus to remain with us after the ascension. Such a view is only a faint reflection of the paschal mystery. The eschatological character of the community, and the central place of mission in its life, also require that the eucharist be situated on a trajectory that begins at baptism, because baptism was and is the disciple's primary experience of the power of Jesus' resurrection.

Consequently, the eucharist must be understood in the context of the formation of a faith-community of disciples, in the context of initiation as a journey in faith and to faith, shared in community. To know what the church is and does, look at what it is and what it does when it gathers people to celebrate the eucharist, for gathering is not limited to the introductory rites of the Mass. During the period of evangelization, inquirers experience the church as herald. During the catechumenate, catechumens experience the church as communion. Those being initiated take on the new identity of church, realized for them in the Easter sacraments of baptism and eucharist. Neophytes, during the mystagogy, reflect on their new character and experience the church as sacrament. Throughout the rest of their lives, they experience the church as servant.

The structural dimension, the church as institution, is experienced at every stage. The church *plans* and *organizes* its proclamation of the word. It is a *structured* community. It has its *visible* side. It *works together* to serve humanity. But when the church presents itself in an authentic fashion, the structural element, though present throughout, is never foremost. Nor is it concentrated on for its own sake: the structure is for the sake of communion, becoming sacrament, heralding, and serving. The same is therefore true of the regulation of ministries, including that of presiding: Regulation is not for the sake of control but for the authenticity of the church.

To prevent a eucharistic ecclesiology from becoming too static and institutional, or too otherworldly and isolated from life, the eucharist must be seen and experienced as the climax of initiation. The necessity of regular eucharistic celebration is then apparent: Because it is in the Easter sacraments that Christians are identified with Christ and take on their identity as the church, they must continue to celebrate the eucharist in order to maintain that identity in its fullness. Christians who realize this truth will not willingly accept eucharistic deprivation.

Catholic terminology normally reserves "local church" for the particular communion headed by a bishop. "Church" as communion, however, is actualized at different levels, though unequally: faith community, eucharistic assembly, regional communion, worldwide communion. Although there is a completeness to a church that includes the episcopal ministry, "church" is by no means a univocal term. It is also realized in the eucharistic assembly and, to a lesser degree, in the noneucharistic Sunday assembly. The ecclesial character of a Sunday assembly without the eucharist, however, requires further investigation,[33] as does the whole theology of the local church. But a basic question is put to us: Because of the part that the eucharist plays in the constitution of church, to what extent can a community unable to celebrate the eucharist be considered church?

Eucharistic Memorial and Christ's Presence

The centrality of the eucharist in the lives of Christians and in the life of the church is not simply because of Christ's presence in the eucharistic meal; simply receiving communion is not enough to identify the community with Christ and give it its identity as church. Were that the case, there would be grounds for arguing that communion from the reserved sacrament is, of itself, sufficient means to achieve the intent of the eucharist. That, however, is not the case. The intent of the eucharist is achievable sacramentally only in the activity of the community as it celebrates the eucharist.

The eucharist is first of all an action, an action of thanksgiving that makes memorial of the paschal mystery. Within the context of that action, Christ's multiple, dynamic presence emerges, of which the eucharistic bread is an enduring sign. It is important, then, to be clear both on the nature of the eucharist as the memorial of the paschal mystery and on the significance of Christ's eucharistic presence.

At his Last Supper, Jesus ritually anticipated his total self-gift on the cross through a prophetic act. He did so by using familiar rituals — sharing bread at the beginning of the meal and drinking a cup of wine at the end — and by giving those rituals new meaning. In addition, his words over the bread and cup did more than give the disciples information. He invited them to engage in an action — to eat and drink — and he challenged them to recognize the new meaning of bread and cup. That new meaning was the creating of a community (specifically, a community of common action) between Jesus and the disciples that would survive his death. He then told them to continue doing these familiar rituals, but to do so now as his memorial (in the Greek of the New Testament, *anamnesis*).

What Jesus meant by memorial was largely determined by the Jewish concept of memorial. Interpretations and explanations of the notion differ, as do the translations of *anamnesis,* but they generally agree that memorial means far more than a souvenir, monument or other remembrance of an action that is over and done with. Memorial is instead a way to experience anew the redemptive word and work of God begun in the past, continuing in the present, and tending toward ultimate fulfillment. Those who make memorial of that word and work of God become present to it. Making memorial was the way the disciples were challenged to share anew in their communion at table the experience of God's redemptive action in the person of Jesus.

Even if Joachim Jeremias is correct in his claim that the Semitic mind understood memorial as bringing God's past salvific action before God so that *God* would "remember" and act to complete the work of salvation,[34] the centrality of action and the continuing experience of redemption remain. In either case, the disciples are challenged to do what Jesus did — to be companions at table in such a way as to share the experience of the reign of God. And as disciples, they are to do this while drawing their life from Christ, who is the redemptive source of a new and everlasting covenant. In this action they would continue to have community with him. Memorial is, thus, far more than a purely subjective remembrance.

The central action was not simply one of sharing a meal. The New Testament does not seem to use "sharing bread" (literally, the breaking of the bread) for common meals, but rather uses it to refer to the special ritual gesture for blessing God that began the Jewish meal. In the post-resurrection communities of Jesus' disciples, this ritual gesture expressed the nature and unity of the church community and may even at times have been used apart from a meal[35] — as, in fact, has come to be the practice in the celebration of the eucharist. The Pauline commentary on the Lord's Supper goes so far as to identify the reality of the church with the *koinonia,* or communion, in the one loaf and one cup. (See 1 Corinthians 10:16 – 17; 11:28 – 29.)

In the New Testament accounts of the Supper, the cup and the sharing of the cup are intimately linked with Jesus' death and the establishment of a new and definitive covenant. The meaning of sharing bread is extended and completed by indicating that there is a means whereby Jesus will maintain communion with his disciples through and beyond his death: All draw their life from a common source, Jesus. But there is the further nuance that such communion requires drinking *his* cup — being committed to self-giving service as he was. Consequently, rather than all the participants having their own cups, as was the usual custom, Jesus gives his cup to be shared by all. The Johannine account of the Supper, which does not speak of the bread and cup rituals, accents this dimension of service with the narrative of washing feet (John 13) and underlines the reality of common life with the presentation of the image of the vine and branches (John 15).

Communion through bread alone lacks the clear indication of these further nuances of service and common source of life. The challenge of total commitment to one another and to all people, which the cup implies, may in fact be one reason for the reluctance to share the common cup. The unavailability of the cup is a further indication of how the communion service lacks an important element of the eucharist. Sharing bread is a comfortable communion. Sharing the cup is not; a person can drink too much and must put his or her lips where others' have been. Drinking Jesus' cup requires living and laying down one's life, as Jesus did, in a service that sets no limits in advance nor excludes anyone but rather takes risks — including the perilous risk of intimacy.

The ritual gestures of sharing bread and cup were, and are, inseparable from blessing God. Even in the face of death, Jesus gave thanks. The thrust of Christian blessing was thanksgiving for what God was accomplishing in and through the person of Jesus. Whatever the ritual origins and structural development of the eucharistic prayer,[36] it clearly interpreted the meaning of gestures that could otherwise be ambiguous: The gestures, in light of the prayer, not only expressed the solidarity of those who had gathered but also their communion in Christ. The memories of the meals taken with Jesus during his ministry, including the Last Supper, were transformed by the continuing experience of communion with the risen Lord even though in time the thanksgiving prayer would give central place to a narrative of the Last Supper as the Christians' charter or mandate for memorializing Jesus in *this* way. The eucharistic prayer thus became the most fundamental way in which the church confessed its faith and committed itself to action.

The eucharistic prayer is not fully intelligible if it is regarded merely as a verbal formula or as something that belongs exclusively to the priest. The eucharistic prayer is inseparable both from the gestures of sharing the bread and the cup and from the sharing of them in common; it is inseparable from the activity of the Body of Christ. It gives words to the action — and to the meaning of the action — of the assembled community. The action is one of thanksgiving (in Greek, *eucharistia*) and bread and the cup take their meaning from this action. To rephrase Justin, it is almost as if the bread and the cup have become the concrete expressions of the community's thanksgiving in union with Jesus' prayer of thanksgiving.

No verbal act of thanksgiving can replace the eucharistic prayer, since any other act of thanksgiving, unlike the eucharistic prayer, is spatially and temporally disconnected from the gestures of sharing the bread and the cup. The gestures are those of another community at another time, and any subsequent prayer of thanksgiving can do no more than refer to them from the outside.

It is the celebration of the eucharist, not the reception of communion, that continues to establish and maintain the reality of the church. Those who have been, and commit to being, identified with Christ, do as he did: They take the bread and cup, bless God, and share the bread and cup. In so doing, they memorialize — become present to and are caught up in the reality of — Jesus' meals during his ministry, his Last Supper and the meals his disciples continued to share with him after Easter. They have communion with Jesus' person and with God's redemptive action, not merely through the reality of Jesus' presence in "transubstantiated" bread and wine but through the reality of his presence in the total reality of the eucharistic *action:* taking, blessing, giving and receiving in a mutual sharing.

The scholastic distinction between the eucharist as sacrament and the eucharist as sacrifice does not imply such a separability in fact. The primacy of the eucharist as action is not at all diminished by the fact that the term "eucharist" is also applied to the gifts over which the eucharistic prayer is spoken. The action of the Spirit-filled community enters into those gifts, but they are "eucharist" only in a derivative fashion and their significance diminishes as they are removed from the action of the community.

This becomes clearer when we recognize that Christ is not present merely in the meal that is to be shared nor in the meal that is actually shared. Christ's manifold presence in the eucharist emerges in the course of the action in which the assembled community engages: gathering in the name of Jesus through song and prayer; listening and responding to the word of God; sharing the experience of God's redemptive action in the Incarnate Word by taking bread and cup, blessing God, and sharing bread and cup; and departing to live a life of service as Christ's Body.[37] Within this multi-faceted realization of Christ's presence, the community and its action hold the primacy because it is toward them that all else is oriented even though the tradition regards Christ's enduring presence in the eucharistic meal as "real" presence.[38]

As we will see in more detail in the next two chapters, the communion service lacks altogether the concrete symbol of continuity and communion with the church through the ages: the ordained presider. In addition, it has only a vestige of the most important symbol — the action of the eucharist — in the form of the eucharistic bread. It consequently fails to present in an adequate manner the mystery of the church that not only does the memorial of the Lord but, in so doing, *becomes* the memorial of the Lord. That memorial is not primarily the substantial presence of Christ in the eucharistic bread and cup, but the experience of God's redemptive action in and through the action of the assembly that does as Jesus did.

Eucharistic Ecclesiology and Communities without Eucharist

As we saw in Chapter One, the inability to celebrate the eucharist, or the conscious decision not to do so, is neither an exclusively modern nor a peculiarly Catholic issue. However, most of the historical instances of communities without the eucharist came from situations where the celebration of the eucharist was more of a clerical function than it was a communal responsibility. It can be argued that this is why the community was little affected when a worship alternative in the form of a devotional service substituted for the eucharist. The community had little involvement in the celebration of the eucharist when it *did* take place. And because what involvement it did have was primarily devotional, the substitution of a devotional service in place of the celebration of the eucharist had little impact on the community.

What is unique in the current situation is that communities that have in recent decades grown accustomed to regular participation in the Sunday celebration of the eucharist are now unable to do so and seem inclined to make the best of a situation over which they have no control.

> Beginning with the late fourth century with abstention from communion on the grounds of awe and unworthiness, the church experienced something new: the split between sacrifice and meal, with people attending the sacrifice but abstaining from the meal. Today we see the opposite: people participating in the meal but not attending the sacrifice. Neither solution is good: both fragment the unified concept of the sacrificial meal.[39]

Will the outcome be a reversion to earlier devotional attitudes and practices? Will ecclesial disintegration result? Or will the need for communities to take responsibility for worship result in an invigoration of celebration and mission?

Both historical precedent and theological reflection suggest that the situation is not merely ambivalent but dangerous. Not surprisingly, the inability to celebrate the eucharist affects the bonds of communion and the experience of church. Where it has already taken place in contemporary Catholicism, the consequences have included less frequent attendance at Sunday worship, less frequent communion, less frequent Easter communion, and a higher number of drop-outs.[40] In some locales, alternative lay ministries have not only substituted for the ordained ministry but have taken communities in the direction of independent sects like the *cofradias* (confraternities) of the Philippines.[41] In Latin America, where the eucharist never became the standard form of Sunday worship, *comunidades de base,* gathering under lay leadership for worship centered on the word, move in the direction of an *iglesia popular* on a congregational model. In addition, large numbers of people have shifted their allegiance to evangelical sects.

If these patterns hold true in the United States, many Catholics deprived of the eucharist will likely leave for other churches, either "liturgical" churches that have only recently rediscovered the importance of Sunday eucharist, or evangelical churches long accustomed to celebrating the word. Some communities will undoubtedly begin to celebrate the eucharist with lay presiders; their ecclesial status will then be suspect, as the broader church will not officially recognize their eucharist or ministry, and they will effectively be in schism. Other communities will, for the most part, grow accustomed to not celebrating the eucharist and will perhaps see little difference as long as they are able to receive communion on occasion.

However many people leave the church, either individually or in groups, the state of those who will remain will be just as problematic. If, in a sacramental church, initiation establishes the sense of church and regular celebration of the eucharist maintains it, then the sense of church in communities without the eucharist will necessarily be affected. Indications are that the ecclesial sense will move in the direction of a congregationalist experience. The bonds of communion between these communities and both the diocesan and worldwide church will weaken. The communion of the diocesan and worldwide church will itself be weakened and distorted.

The reason is simple. As a communion, the church has both invisible and visible elements. Invisibly, ecclesial communion is a common life with God through Christ in the Spirit. Visibly, this common life is mediated both sacramentally and structurally or institutionally: Baptism and the eucharist mediate the common life sacramentally; structures of communication, mutuality, and co-operation mediate it institutionally.

But since these two means of mediation interrelate and complement one another, as one means diminishes the other is distorted. Without the eucharist, the institutional element of communion is likely to move in the direction of either control and restriction or benign neglect. In either case, the least desirable features of the institutional model of church will be increasingly obvious and will lead to either greater rigidity or disintegration. The role of the ordained presider, a role that links the sacramental and institutional expressions of communion, is thus a key element in the celebration of the eucharist, even apart from the outmoded theology of a "power to confect" received in ordination.

Without the eucharist, the bonds of ecclesial communion are likely to be lost or to become shackles. If SWAP is significantly less than the eucharist, a church dependent upon it for expressing and effecting its faith will necessarily be weakened because of the distorted faith that is the consequence. Since ritual is the primary means of handing on the tradition of the Christian experience, the experience is distorted if the ritual is distorted. As the U.S. bishops have noted: "Faith grows when it is well expressed in celebration. Good celebrations foster and nourish faith. Poor celebrations weaken and destroy faith."[42]

To obviate this danger, parishes without ordained pastors are provided with delegated lay leaders, and preconsecrated bread is put on their tables. The attempt, clearly, is to maintain visible bonds of communion to mediate the common life both institutionally and sacramentally. And the common life does continue to be so mediated, but in a diminished manner— through leaders delegated by the bishop, but not ordained, and through presanctified bread. (Awareness of the weakening of ecclesial and sacramental communion when the communion service replaces the eucharist leads the *Directory* to affirm the customary practice of having a verbal statement of communion. Such a statement would include elements that attempt to connect the community that is holding a communion service with the broader church; e.g., references to where the priest is celebrating that day and what community shared its eucharist to provide the presanctified bread.[43]) What is lost is the intimate relationship between pastoral and eucharistic leadership as well as the sense of the eucharist as a community activity. Pastoral leaders are not authorized to preside at the eucharist, and the priest who presides at the eucharist when it is celebrated may be a stranger to the community's life. The eucharist becomes again a thing that is individually received rather than an activity in which the community realizes itself as the Body of Christ. This is hardly the dynamic orientation to communion and mission that the eucharist is supposed to be.

The weakening of ecclesial communion is not merely a future threat. The absence of Sunday eucharist, less frequent Sunday eucharist or even diminished participation in the celebration are themselves symptoms that the church has begun to lose its cohesion. Periods of history when lay participation became passive or when the frequency of communion declined provide evidence for that. Granted, even without full, active, communal participation, the eucharistic ritual still has power to express and maintain institutional cohesion, a sense of communion and a sense of community.[44] Granted, even without the eucharist God is able to accomplish what the eucharist is oriented toward — the communion of Christians in Christ. But the centrality of the eucharist for maintaining and expressing the identification of communities with Jesus means that we risk entering a vicious circle: A weakened ecclesial communion leads us to tolerate SWAP in place of the eucharist, and the lack of the eucharist leads us in the direction of a further weakening of communion.

No alternative, not even communion outside Mass, is as expressive of ecclesial communion as is the eucharist. The intimate relationship between church and eucharist began in the meals Jesus shared with sinners, was raised to a new level at the Last Supper when Jesus, facing death, challenged his disciples to do tablesharing and service as his memorial, and became essential after Easter to maintain the church in Jesus' Spirit. Jesus' disciples again become church as they do the eucharist, for in their twofold activity of doing Jesus' memorial and knowing his presence in the breaking of bread, they are the ones in whom the Spirit dwells.

Thus, eucharistic ecclesiology not only indicates where the church is to be found but also underlines that the church needs the eucharist to be church and to do what church does. Even with communion from the reserved sacrament, SWAP is unable to do what the eucharist does for the church: to give impetus to sacramental living and to effect transformation into sacrament so that the church can fulfill its mission. It is unable because, though the disciples know the presence of the Lord in the reserved sacrament, they do not engage in doing his memorial. Without that twofold activity they are not, as a community, filled with his Spirit to be sacrament of the church. Without that twofold activity, ecclesial communion is weakened. The risk is that Sunday worship without the eucharist will weaken the bonds between communities and that communities reduced to SWAP will forget the broader church and its communion through the ages.

Chapter Three
Endnotes

1. This statement had strong support in the undivided church of the first millennium, as did the Church's nature as communion. For an examination of Catholic and Orthodox studies, see Paul McPartlan, *The Eucharist Makes the Church: Henri de Lubac and John Zizioulas in Dialogue* (Edinburgh: T & T Clark, 1993).

2. Alexander Schmemann, *The Eucharist: Sacrament of the Kingdom* (Crestwood, NY: St. Vladimir's Seminary Press, 1987), 11.

3. See Jerome Hamer, *The Church Is a Communion* (New York: Sheed and Ward, 1962), 13–17.

4. See especially Emile Mersch, *The Theology of the Mystical Body* (St. Louis: B. Herder, 1951). See also Otto Semmelroth, *Die Kirche als Ursakrament* (Frankfurt: J. Knecht, 1953).

5. For a detailed study, see Oskar Saier, *"Communio" in der Lehre des zweiten Vatikanischen Konzils: Eine rechtsbegriffliche Untersuchung,* Münchener Theologische Studien, Kanonistische Abteilung, b. 32 (München: Max Hueber Verlag, 1973).

6. Joseph Ratzinger, *Church, Ecumenism and Politics* (New York: Crossroad, 1988), 7. The 1985 Extraordinary Synod, in its final document, spoke of communion as the most central and fundamental idea in the Vatican II documents and the key to renewing Catholic ecclesiology. This centrality was reaffirmed by the Congregation for the Doctrine of the Faith in its "Letter to the Bishops of the Catholic Church on Some Aspects of the Church Understood as Communion." See *Origins* 22 (1992): 108.

7. Vatican II, *Dogmatic Constitution on the Church (Lumen gentium)* [hereafter LG] (November 21, 1964), no. 1.

8. See, for example, Bernard Cooke, *Sacraments and Sacramentality* (Mystic, CT: Twenty-Third Publications, 1983). For a more technical and detailed study, see his *The Distancing of God: The Ambiguity of Symbol in History and Theology* (Minneapolis: Fortress, 1990).

9. For a brief report, see Andrew Greeley, "Sacraments keep Catholics high on the Church," *National Catholic Reporter* (April 12, 1991): 12–13.

10. Henri de Lubac, *Corpus Mysticum: L'eucharistie et l'Église au moyen âge: Etude historique,* 2d ed. (Paris: Aubier, 1949).

11. See 1 Corinthians 11:17–34, though 1 Corinthians 12–14 is obviously a further consideration of the same issue. For a discussion of the interrelationship of community and the eucharist in Paul's understanding, see Jerome Murphy-O'Connor, "Eucharist and Community in First Corinthians," *Worship* 50 (1976): 370–85; 51 (1977): 56–69.

12. See William R. Crockett, *Eucharist: Symbol of Transformation* (New York: Pueblo, 1989), 29–34.

13. See especially excerpts in Daniel J. Sheerin, ed., *The Eucharist,* Message of the Fathers of the Church, vol. 7 (Collegeville: The Liturgical Press/Michael Glazier, 1986), 93–108. Similar themes are found in the fourth-century mystagogia; see Edward Yarnold, *The Awe-Inspiring Rites of Initiation: Baptismal Homilies of the Fourth Century* (Slough: St. Paul Publications, 1971).

14. E.g., *Summa Theologica,* III, q. 73, a. 3, resp.

15. Bernard Leeming, *Principles of Sacramental Theology,* 2nd. ed. (Westminster, MD: Newman Press, 1960), 255.

16. For a detailed examination of the development, see Gary Macy, *The Theologies of the Eucharist in the Early Scholastic Period* (New York: Oxford University Press, 1984). For the historical development of the distinctions, see Ronald F. King, "The Origin and Development of a Sacramental Formula: *Sacramentum Tantum, Res et Sacramentum, Res Tantum,*" *The Thomist* 31 (1967): 21–82.

17. See SC, no. 14.

18. Wilhelm de Vries, among others, has provided this corrective to Afanassiev's views. See his "Unterschiedliche Kirchenbilder im Ost und West im blick auf eine eucharistische Ekklesiologie" in Albert Rauch and Paul Imhof, eds., *Die Eucharistie der Einen Kirche: Eucharistische Ekklesiologie — Perspektiven und Grenzen* (Munich: Verlagsgesellschaft Gerrhard Kaffke, 1983), 51–71. Almost all the essays in this collection are worth examining. I have reviewed it and indicated the contents of the individual essays in *Journal of Ecumenical Studies* 23 (1986): 146–47.

19. See, for example, the 1982 Catholic-Orthodox joint statement, "The Mystery of the Church and the Eucharist in Light of the Mystery of the Holy Trinity," *Origins* 12 (1982): 157–60.

20. For a collection of texts and an introductory explanation, see A. Hamman, ed., *The Paschal Mystery: Ancient Liturgies and Patristic Texts* (Staten Island, NY: Alba House,1969).

21. LG, no. 26.

22. LG lends itself to this interpretation in several places, even though its perspective is clearly "from the top down"; see especially nos. 23 and 26.

23. *Ecclesiogenesis,* 19–20. Among others, Karl Rahner also argues that the very existence of such a community carries with it the right to be recognized as church; see his *The Shape of the Church to Come,* 109.

24. See SC, nos. 2, 26, 41, 42; LG, nos. 3, 7, 10, 11, 23, 26, 28, 50.

25. EM, no. 7 [DOL 179, no. 1236].

26. See Congregation for the Doctrine of the Faith, "Letter to the Bishops of the Catholic Church on Some Aspects of the Church Understood as Communion," *Origins* 22 (1992), 110.

27. LG, no. 23.

28. Congregation for the Doctrine of the Faith, "Letter to the Bishops of the Catholic Church on Some Aspects of the Church Understood as Communion," *Origins* 22 (1992), 110.

29. *Ibid.,* 109.

30. *De unitate,* no. 5.

31. *Ep.* 43, 5, 2. I have used the translation found in G. W. Clarke, trans. and ed., *The Letters of St. Cyprian of Carthage,* v. 2, *Ancient Christian Writers,* v. 44, (New York: Newman Press, 1984), 64.

32. *Letter to the Smyrnaeans,* 8, in *Ancient Christian Writers,* v. 1, p. 93.

33. See Pierre-Andrè Liégé, "Accompagnement Ecclésiologique pour les Assemblées Dominicales sans Célébration Eucharistique," *La Maison-Dieu* 130 (1977): 128–144.

34. *The Eucharistic Words of Jesus* (London: SCM, 1966), 237–255.

35. David N. Power, *The Eucharistic Mystery: Revitalizing the Tradition* (New York: Crossroad, 1992), 72ff.

36. See especially Louis Bouyer, *Eucharist: Theology and Spirituality of the Eucharistic Prayer* (Notre Dame: University of Notre Dame Press, 1968). David Power surveys subsequent research in his *The Eucharistic Mystery,* passim.

37. For statements of the varied manner of Christ's presence, see especially *Mediator Dei;* SC, no. 7; *Mysterium fidei,* nos. 35–39 [DOL 176, nos. 1179–1183]; EM, no. 9 [DOL 179, no. 1238]; GIRM, no. 7 [DOL 208, no. 1397]. Note that *Mysterium fidei* and *Eucharisticum mysterium* reverse the order of *Sacrosanctum concilium* and begin with Christ's presence in the community rather than with Christ's presence in the eucharistic meal. This approach is more conducive to seeing the celebration as the dynamic unfolding of Christ's manifold presence.

38. For a comprehensive, though tendentious, study of this tradition, see Jean-Charles Didier, *Histoire de la Présence Réelle* (Paris: Éditions C.L.D., 1978).

39. Gerard Austin, "Communion Services," 213.

40. See Kerkhofs, *Concilium* 133 (1980): 3–11. Yet the data gathered by Brulin, "Les assemblées dominicales," do not indicate so precipitous a decline.

41. See Duschak, "Sunday Services," 262.

42. *Music in Catholic Worship* (Washington, DC: United States Catholic Conference, 1972), no. 6.

43. Directory, no. 43.

44. See John Bossy, "The Mass as a Social Institution, 1200–1700," *Past and Present* 100 (1983): 29–61. Much more detail is provided in his *Christianity in the West, 1400–1700* (New York: Oxford University Press, 1985).

The Eucharistic Sacrifice and the Communion Service

Communities prevented from celebrating Sunday eucharist do suffer harm from this deprivation. They suffer because SWAP is not the eucharist: It is not the memorial of the Lord's paschal mystery. We have already seen one effect, the weakening of ecclesial communion. But the more radical effect is the consequence of communities being unable to share fully in the eucharistic sacrifice. The eucharist is not, first and foremost, the presence of the Lord in consecrated bread and wine but the celebration of the paschal or Easter mystery, the Lord's dying and rising — what the tradition calls his "sacrifice" and to which we are present in the celebration of the eucharist. This difference between the eucharist and SWAP — the diminishment of the sacrificial dimension — will occupy our attention in this chapter.

While the Roman *Directory* states that a clear distinction exists between the eucharistic sacrifice and the communion service, it could leave the impression that, from the laity's perspective, the only difference is the priest's absence.[1] The need for the thanksgiving to be altogether different in form from the eucharistic prayer (45) closely correlates with the priest's absence, leaving the impression that the eucharistic prayer

87

belongs exclusively to the priest. The importance of the priest's role in the Mass is frequently reiterated throughout the document, as is the statement that the communion service is not to be confused with the Mass. All of this gives the impression that the assembly's only involvement in the eucharistic sacrifice is the reception of communion. Thus, its participation in the communion service is little different from its participation in the eucharist: In both cases the "fruits" are still received (32).[2] The impression that is left is that people lose little by having the communion service rather than Mass.

In communities where the liturgical reforms of the Second Vatican Council have been only partially implemented, or where people have not been helped to reflect upon their significance as an assembly, the difference may seem minimal. SWAP is merely a "priestless Mass" and people may, in fact, prefer "Sister's Mass." Where the attempt is made to keep SWAP as similar to the eucharist as possible — especially by including a prayer of thanksgiving and communion from the reserved sacrament — the two are structurally almost indistinguishable. However, this may be both dishonest and more dangerous than highlighting the differences: To the extent that the communion service appears adequate and complete, it will lessen the felt need for the eucharist[3] and will make the situation seem normal.

We have already seen that the eucharistic prayer does more than simply verbally state the community's gratitude for what God has done in Christ. As a memorial sacrifice of thanksgiving, the eucharist is an action manifesting the paschal mystery. Thus, the broader significance of the eucharistic prayer is that it states the meaning of what the assembly *does* in thanksgiving: It identifies with Christ by doing what he did, both at table and in service. The prayer of thanksgiving in SWAP, as we have also seen, is limited to a verbal statement — because it is extrinsic to the gestures whereby the assembly identifies with Christ — and can easily become a derivative, devotional statement centered on the eucharistic bread supplied by an earlier celebration or by another community.

Protestant traditions have often included a prayer of thanksgiving in noneucharistic services. How this has been structured and how it relates to the eucharistic prayer could be instructive. Generally, however, such prayers have been linked with the collection, because reservation of the eucharist and communion from the reserved sacrament normally have not been practiced.

The inclusion of an act of thanksgiving in the communion service does more than simply provide a structural parallel to the eucharistic prayer. It maintains a eucharistic orientation beyond the reception of communion by including in the Sunday worship a thanksgiving to God for redemption in Christ. To this extent, the prayer of thanksgiving is good. Thanksgiving is a central element of Christian worship and it does need to be expressed, even if a community cannot celebrate the eucharist, which is the appropriate way of giving thanks.[4] But adding this element is not enough to enable the communion service to do what the eucharist does. Adding this prayer of thanksgiving may even confuse if it helps lead to the conclusion that receiving communion in the eucharist and receiving communion in the communion service are no different from each other.

Some differences between the eucharist and the communion service are ceremonial. Others are liturgical and theological. But for the most part — as would be expected — these are inseparable because in liturgy, ceremony is generally a concrete presentation of theology. Is it significant, for example, if the lay presider uses a different chair than the priest does, if words substitute for symbols, or if the structure consistently parallels the Sunday eucharist but lacks its central dynamics? The eucharist and the communion service seem almost alike. Nevertheless, they differ significantly when viewed from the perspective of the community realizing in a sacramental way Christ's redemptive sacrifice through its activity of doing the Lord's memorial and knowing his presence as they do so.

The Eucharist As Sacrifice[5]

Despite the negative connotations of "sacrifice" in modern usage, the concept remains deeply embedded in the Christian faith as a means of characterizing Christ's redemptive self-gift. "Sacrifice" has also been a key element of Catholic eucharistic theology, which regards the eucharistic action as the

89

sacrament of Christ's all-sufficient offering. Its absence is the single most obvious difference between the eucharist and the communion service. Appreciating the significance of its absence requires some attention to the character of the eucharist as sacrifice and to the manner in which this is ritualized.

In speaking of the eucharist as sacrifice, it is first necessary to recognize that the New Testament reverses the usual understanding of sacrifice. The notion of sacrifice had already undergone extensive spiritualization in Judaism by the first century CE, but sacrifice was still often understood as the offering made by people to God. Christ's sacrifice, however, is not primarily something that goes from humans to God but rather from God to humans. In this way it shows that God is for us. What humanity cannot achieve, God accomplishes for us. This redemptive presence of God is called "sacrifice" because it is the gift that accomplishes the communion of life between God and humanity intended but never accomplished by cultic sacrifices. The communion of life, not material offering, is essential to sacrifice.[6] This metaphorical usage reverses the usual understanding of sacrifice. As God's human presence, Christ is God's self-communication as life for us. Nevertheless, God does not do this for us without us: As human and representative of humanity, Christ offers himself, and us with him, to God on our behalf.

Participating in Christ's Sacrifice

Christ's sacrifice is memorialized in the shape of a meal to be shared in thanksgiving to God. The confusion of the dogmatic (vebal reflection) and liturgical (ritual action) modes of speech, coupled with the fact that only the priest (generally assisted by other ministers) was actively involved in the essential actions of the liturgy, led to identifying the eucharistic sacrifice with a specific element of the eucharistic liturgy. We need to clarify the interrelation beween these two modes of speech — between theological reflection and ritual action — in order to clarify the significance of the eucharist as sacrifice and the inability of the communion service to compensate for the lack of the sacrificial dimension.

Within the restricted experience of the medieval clerical eucharist, theology came to see the physical essence of the sacrifice in the double consecration performed by the priest. That the eucharist is sacrifice — a dogmatic statement — was thus seen as realized in a specific liturgical element where only the priest appeared to be actively involved on the level of ritual. The uncritical acceptance of the outlook shaped by the allegorical interpretations of the Mass undoubtedly played a major part in the prehistory of the scholastic position. These allegorical interpretations were attempts to interpret liturgical ritual by applying a meaning from outside the liturgy: Spectators at Mass were taught to see a correspondence between the priest's actions at Mass and the events of Christ's life, especially his suffering and death. "Body" and "Blood" were regarded as separate from one another — despite the later doctrine of concomitance — as a sign of Christ's death, which in turn was regarded as essential to sacrifice.

Adherents of this view failed to differentiate between dogmatic and theological understanding (sacrifice) on the one hand, and liturgical ritual (the signs of bread and wine dealt with separately) on the other. It is important to distinguish dogmatic and liturgical modes of speech. On the level of dogma, the eucharist is the sacrament of Christ's historical passion and death and the sacrament of his eternal offering of that sacrifice. On the level of liturgy, the eucharist is the church's activity and is thus the sacrifice of the church. When the historical offering and the liturgical offering are confused, they are as likely to be identified as to be regarded independently. In either case, the nature of sacrament is threatened.

The scholastics confused these two modes of speech largely because they were unaware of the Jewish origins of the Christian eucharist, especially the centrality of the meal within the sacrifice. As a consequence, they considered the priest as able to offer the sacrifice without any need whatsoever of the assembly's participation. The major means of lay participation was the reception of communion, which gradually grew in frequency following the Council of Trent but did not begin to approximate that of the early centuries until after the Second Vatican Council.

The scholastics not only failed to distinguish between dogmatic understanding and liturgical ritual, but also failed to distinguish between history and liturgy. Christ's sacrifice was historically made once and for all, even if it is eternalized in his active human presence within the Trinity. The priest's role is liturgical, and the priest acts in the person of Christ (in persona Christi) on the level of liturgical rite, not on the level of theological reality. He does not take the place of the absent Christ: Christ in the Spirit is inwardly present to the community and is present in the community's sacramental activity. The priest memorializes that presence through his actions as chief host, heading the table and voicing the prayer.

The Tridentine insistence that the eucharist is sacrifice in the same sense as Christ's sacrifice, though in an unbloody manner,[7] means that all that is new in the sacrifice of the Mass is our participation. Thus, a theology that sees sacrifice realized in the consecration of bread and wine must be broadened to see the whole eucharistic prayer, not just Jesus' words at the Last Supper, as consecratory. It must also broaden its perspective to see that it is not only the eucharistic prayer but also the entire liturgy of the eucharist that memorializes the paschal mystery and is thus consecratory. Ritual activity is itself prayer and has priority over words, even though the eucharistic prayer is the necessary wording of the activity's meaning. Because ritual prayer consecrates both the assembly and its meal, we must pay attention to the manner in which the assembly's participation in Christ's sacrifice is actualized in and through its liturgical activity. The assembly's participation in the ritual prayer extends beyond merely receiving communion.

The whole eucharistic prayer is consecratory because it expresses the meaning and significance of the assembly and its meal as both are drawn into Christ's destiny. In the eucharist, the church's prayer of praise and thanksgiving is especially for what God has accomplished through the Crucified and Risen One, and its intercession is for all those for whom his life is given. More than mere words, this prayer is a ritual identification with Christ and a commitment to his mission by being one with his prayer. Gathered as Christ's Body at table, the community's prayer is one with his as he offered praise and thanks in the face of death at the Last Supper, and as he offers it forever at the banquet table of the heavenly liturgy. This is most clearly expressed in the epiclesis, the invocation of the

Spirit — split in the Roman and Alexandrian traditions into consecratory and communion epicleses — and the intercessions.

The minimal expression of the epiclesis in the Roman Canon is the reason the Orthodox church questions the validity of the Roman eucharist. Neglecting the epiclesis correlates with the focus on the priest's liturgical activity — the separate consecration of the bread and wine — as the physical essence of the eucharistic sacrifice. The epiclesis in the Roman Canon is almost exclusively consecratory — an invocation of the Spirit to consecrate the gifts — and barely suggests the communion-character, the consecration of the community. This parallels Western clericalism and the West's misplaced focus on the eucharistic elements and their transformation. When the Spirit's role in the social drama of the eucharist does not receive explicit attention, both the actor who takes the part of Christ by repeating his words and the props that the actor holds achieve undue prominence at the expense of the assembled Body of Christ. A broadened understanding of the epiclesis is based upon the realization that it is Christ — symbolized first by the assembly and then, because of his role, by the priest — who is present both in the Spirit to transform the church into his Body and within that context to transform the meal that will be set before them. The intercessions that flow from the communion epiclesis make clear that Christ's presence in the eucharistic meal *(res et sacramentum)* is oriented to Christ's presence in his community-Body *(res sacramenti)* so that Christ may continue to serve the needs of humanity.

Likewise, the meaning of the eucharist is truncated if reference is made only to the Last Supper. This mistake was made ritually by the sixteenth-century Protestant reformers who retained only the institution narrative from the eucharistic prayer. It was made theologically by Catholic theologians who adverted almost exclusively to the priest's role (taking Christ's part at the Last Supper) and the "words of consecration" (the repetition of Christ's "key" words at the Last Supper). Though there is a continuity in form between the eucharist and the Last Supper (and likewise a continuity with the meals of the ministry and the meals of the risen Lord), a discontinuity is introduced by the resurrection. The resurrection of Jesus in the Spirit is a new presence to his disciples. From this perspective, the church is part of what happened to Jesus in the resurrection and therefore is inseparable from him. The assembled community, as a fuller sacrament of Christ and of the church, is that presence of Christ because it prays for that presence in his Spirit.

Not the priest alone, then, but the community as a whole, (including the priest functioning sacramentally in relation to Christ and the community) offers the sacrifice. This should be acknowledged and expressed, both theologically and liturgically. Thus the Second Vatican Council states that Christian believers attending the mystery of faith should not do so as though they were outsiders or silent onlookers. Rather, "they should learn to offer themselves as they offer the immaculate victim — not just through the hands of the priest, but also they themselves making the offering together with him."[8] In speaking of the relationship between the common priesthood and the ministerial priesthood, Vatican II says that "the faithful . . . by virtue of their royal priesthood, join in the offering of the eucharist."[9] These statements, in context, go beyond Pius XII's more limited expression in *Mediator Dei*.[10] Pius' affirmation that the faithful join in the offering is marked by numerous qualifications, cautions and warnings because he saw the essence of the sacrifice in the words of consecration, which only the priest performs (92). He saw the assembly's offering of the sacrifice primarily in terms of participation in the priest's offering of the sacrifice — participation through dialogue, presenting bread and wine, and giving a stipend (90) — and in offering it in union with the priest, uniting their hearts with the prayers of the priest (93).

The assembly actualizes its participation in Christ's sacrifice, its entering into Christ's destiny and self-offering, by its celebration of the *full* eucharistic ritual. The reception of communion, which can be an experience of passivity and dependence, is not enough to express the assembly's role in offering the sacrifice.[11] As Gregory Dix pointed out, the ritual as a whole maintains the shape or basic pattern of Christ's table hospitality.[12] That basic pattern is found in the meals of Jesus' ministry, the Last Supper and the meals of the risen Christ. But the same pattern is evident in the eucharist only when the assembled community celebrates the full range of its dynamics.

As the Body of Christ present here and now, the assembly — not just the priest — does what Jesus did. It takes bread and cup, blesses God, breaks the bread, and shares the bread and cup, expressing and effecting mutual service as well as a commitment to the service of God and the world. Each of these actions is important because each is part of the ritual meal by which Jesus prophetically enacted his message, anticipated his death and shared his risen life with his disciples. Each should be developed theologically and liturgically so that it is apparent that each is the action of the community.

The assembly takes bread and cup. It does so by preparing the altar and the gifts. Its involvement in this activity is clear when members of the assembly present the gifts or set the table, especially when some of them have actually baked the bread and brought the bread and wine. The assembly's involvement is less evident when only the priest prepares the altar and gifts. In such an instance, the assembly only sings accompaniment, verbally responds to the prayers or watches mutely.

The assembly blesses God. The theological and ritual highpoint of the assembly's participation in Christ's sacrifice is the eucharistic prayer. At his Last Supper, in the face of death, Jesus gave thanks and consecrated himself to completing his mission. Because the eucharistic prayer makes explicit the link between the assembly's present activity and Christ's redemptive act, it is the assembly's prayer, even if it is voiced by the presider. This theological truism should be ritually apparent.[13] It is clearer when the assembly sings the eucharistic acclamations and even more so when there are recurring refrains that are sung during the prayer. Interestingly, congregations often have more involvement in SWAP's prayers of thanksgiving than they do in the eucharistic prayer! And yet it is the eucharistic prayer that is the prayer of the assembled community.

The assembly breaks bread. The breaking of bread actually initiates the sharing and should not be regarded as an independent ritual action (as was the case in the allegorical interpretations of the Mass). Xavier Léon-Dufour has pointed out that the scriptural *klasis tou artou* is more accurately translated as "sharing bread."[14] The advantage, he says, is twofold. First, "sharing bread" more clearly encompasses the entire ritual action that began the Jewish religious meal and expressed its significance. Second, "sharing bread" includes reference to the kind of life normally symbolized by ritual participation: a life of sharing. The assembly's involvement is clearer if, as the Sacramentary insists, the bread is large enough to be broken and shared.[15] It is also clearer if lay ministers take part in the breaking and giving, whether ordained ministers are available or not.

The assembly shares the bread and the cup. Entering fully into Christ's destiny and self-offering requires sharing the meal, for the sacrament — dining together — is not finished until it is shared. How it is shared should symbolize and embody commitment to the community's mutual and outgoing service. Coming forward is the ritual equivalent to the altar call in evangelical churches: a public act of commitment. Receiving both the bread and the cup in one's hands — not receiving the bread on the tongue or merely touching the chalice with one's lips as the minister holds it — expresses an active, responsive acceptance of God's gift. Bread that must be chewed, along with the common cup, ensure that communion is the action of eating and drinking.

The active involvement of the assembly in this complex of actions that shapes the eucharist expresses and effects mutual service and commitment to the service of God and world. But participation in Christ's sacrifice requires not only the activity of the assembled community; it also requires the entire ritual shape. The entire eucharistic meal, from start to finish, is necessary to express ritually what is stated theologically in terms of sacrifice. One part of the ritual cannot carry the full weight of meaning alone, any more than one member of the community is able to commit the entire community.

This is evident when the rhythm and the relative importance of the ritual elements are made explicit: *Taking* the bread and the cup is for the sake of *blessing* God, and *breaking* the bread is for the sake of *sharing* the bread and the cup. Each part must be viewed as being part of the rhythm of a complex ritual and not as an independent action.

The "taking," however expressed, must not be isolated as an independent expression of self-oblation. Dix understood the offertory rite as each worshiper's act of self-sacrifice. Though scholars question this interpretation, it has influenced popular understanding. The presentation of the gifts and the receiving of communion are often regarded as the people's ritual participation in the offering of the sacrifice. In this view, the presentation of bread and wine represents either the people's offering of themselves to God or the spiritual sacrifices of their lives. While Dix's view here is less distorted than the one that focuses on the "moment of consecration" (especially the separate consecration) as the realization of the sacrifice, it is still inadequate.[16] Nor is the presentation of bread and wine the offering that the people make to God, while the priest presents Christ's self-offering to God. The risk is that the people's offering, whether of bread and wine or of themselves, could be regarded as something added alongside Christ's offering of himself.

The error at the root of the misunderstanding that the "taking" is a self-offering independent of the rest of the ritual is an exaggerated need to differentiate the liturgical roles of priest and laity. Thus, if this is the laity's offering, then the essence of the sacrificial action — the consecration — belongs solely to the priest and the sacrifice is fully completed even if the priest alone shares communion. To isolate laity and priest from one another in this fashion is to threaten the integrity and sufficiency of Christ's sacrifice.

The "blessing" — of God, not of bread and wine — is broader than the consecration of bread and wine. Just as Jesus consecrated himself in the meals he shared, especially at the Last Supper, the eucharistic prayer consecrates the assembly of the faithful by uniting them with the prayer and action of Christ. This is a ritual and theological highpoint because it is the verbal interpretation of the meaning of the assembly's activity. Yet this alone is not the sacrifice, because it is primarily words rather than action.

"Breaking" was a focal point for the realization of sacrifice in the allegorical interpretations. Since death was regarded as the essence of sacrifice, it had to be ritually expressed. The separate consecration of bread and wine was seen as a sign of Christ's death, as was the breaking of the bread. However, a knowledge of the Jewish origins of the Christian eucharist shows that these ritual elements were not intended to dramatize Jesus' death. Deeper theological analysis shows that the concept of sacrifice is broader than death. This is not to deny that Jesus' death is sacrifice; what is required is a more adequate understanding of sacrifice and a clarification of how sacrificial imagery has been used to refer to the death of Jesus. Even more significantly, the fact that cult language ("sacrifice") was used to refer to what was *not* cult (Jesus' death) means that the liturgical usage of sacrificial language must lead participants beyond ritual to a way of life.[17] The breaking of the loaf of bread "dramatizes" the life of sharing to which Jesus' disciples are called. It is through such a life that the disciples proclaim the death of the Lord until he comes.

"Sharing" is also a ritual and theological highpoint. However, the meaning of "sharing" is ambivalent without the interpretation provided by the assembly's participation in the prayer over the bread and cup as the sequel to its taking the bread and cup. "Meal to be shared" (sacrament) and "shared meal" (liturgical completion of the sacrifice) are necessarily connected and mutually implied: The intention that the meal be shared must be realized in actual sharing to complete the sacrifice. Communion that looks to being "alone with Jesus" is *not* fully communion; it is a Corinthian communion that fails to recognize the Body.

It is not just that these four actions — taking, blessing, breaking and sharing — are the ritual shape of the eucharist. Involvement in them is also the means whereby the assembly is associated with Jesus' sacrifice here and now. The metaphor of sacrifice may seem irrelevant in a culture where sacrifices are not offered. Yet the scapegoating tendency and the modern ritualization of violence as a means of catharsis — as can be seen in contemporary drama, music, novels, sports, and even cartoons — shows that sacrificial imagery still has relevance.

The doctrine of Jesus' death as sacrifice comes from the earliest stages of Christianity and may indeed be traceable to the sayings of Jesus.[18] Such a doctrine was necessary for seeing the Temple cult as being fulfilled and abrogated, as is clearly taught in Romans and Hebrews. But Old Testament sacrificial references to the death of Jesus cannot be applied without incorporating the eschatological fulfillment of the resurrection. Not to do so would leave such application without a credible foundation and the resurrection itself with only apologetic or compensatory significance. Thus, the doctrine of the soteriological character of the death of Jesus of Nazareth is included in the primal event that originated Christian faith, the eschatological event of the resurrection. This does not mean, however, that sacrificial imagery implies a particular theory of atonement, whether objective (the penal substitution theory of Anselm, favored by conservatives) or subjective (the faith-response to God's demonstration of love, as Abelard understood it and as preferred by liberals). Such a dichotomy needs to be transcended.[19]

The use of cult language for what is not cult also requires us to go beyond the individualistic context in which atonement has generally been placed and to see that worship, service and atonement were and are inseparable. The (at least) weekly post-Easter celebration of the eucharist was probably originally understood as a sacrificial meal of the Risen Lord akin to the *todah* or thanksgiving sacrifice. This was not a Passover meal celebrated more frequently than once a year but rather a Lord's Day meal of the Risen One whereby his disciples proclaimed "the Lord's death until he comes" (1 Corinthians 11:26). They did this by making liturgical memorial *(anamnesis)* of God's saving presence in Christ's death as they gave thanks. In 1 Corinthians 11, Paul makes clear that this involves much more than merely eating and drinking as a ritual performance.

The eucharist today is neither the making of a new offering to God nor a receiving of the benefits of Christ's offering. It is rather "the realization of God's act of atonement in and for the worshipers."[20] Of course, if there is no commitment to mission, we have only the symbol of a symbol, not an actualization. On the other hand, while the word of God can move people to work for justice, the eucharist provides them with a concrete experience of justice in the reign of God. As Robert Hovda put it, the liturgy is a parable in action.

> Parables do not argue laboriously from where we are to where we should eventually be. Parables take us by the hair of our heads and put us in new situations where we feel new demands and have to make new decisions. What parable is in preaching and verbal teaching, liturgy is in the realm of group action. And that is what good celebration does. Good celebration of liturgy makes no

effort to start where we are. It doesn't try to look like this drab Anglo culture most of us are stuck in, with its preoccupation with words and its constipated suspicion of the senses. Good liturgical celebration, like a parable, takes us by the hair of our heads and puts us in a king-domscene, where we are treated like we've never been treated before . . . because this is clearly and intentionally God's domain, God's reign . . . where we are bowed to and incensed and sprinkled and kissed and touched and fed with a bread and a cup that are equally shared among all. It's a whole new scene. And it prompts some beautiful new feelings. And it calls for some beautiful new decisions.[21]

Can all this happen in a service that depends almost solely on words? Can the justice orientation of the eucharist be experienced in a communion service?

Inadequacy of Communion Service

The activity of sharing the meal is ambivalent without the interpretation given when the assembly is present for, and clearly participates in, the prayer over the bread and the cup. This point is crucial to seeing why SWAP, even with a prayer of thanksgiving and with communion from the reserved sacrament, is insufficient to express full participation in Christ's sacrifice.

Certainly, a verbal statement alone is insufficient. Interpretation separated from the activity interpreted is a faulty sacrament. Action, including an orientation to service, is a fuller interpretation than words. But the assembly's activity in the prayer of thanksgiving and in communion from the reserved sacrament is likewise inadequate in comparison with the eucharistic ideal.

Adding a prayer of thanksgiving is not merely a means of making a non-eucharistic liturgy sound like the eucharist. It does indeed enable the assembly to give thanks to God for salvation in Christ. And to the extent that the assembly's mutual acceptance, showing of hospitality, and commitment to service are actually expressed as well, such a prayer does make a verbal link between Christ and the assembly's worship.

100

It does, therefore, certainly express that the communion service has a eucharistic character, though that is hardly likely to be questioned in any case.

What the prayer of thanksgiving lacks, however, is not merely the institution narrative or "words of consecration." Some ancient eucharistic prayers lacked this, too. What is missing is the organic unity between the sacrificial intention and the sacrificial meal. This is achieved only in the continuity of a single assembly engaged in the full eucharistic action.

Praying a prayer of thanksgiving is not enough. While it does express the community's gratitude, the community realizes that its thanksgiving is more derivative from another celebration than constitutive of its own reality. In addition, there is the risk that the prayer will be oriented more to giving thanks for the meal than for God's action in Christ.

Communion from the reserved sacrament is a means of participation in the eucharistic sacrifice. From ancient times, since at least the middle of the second century, communion has been shared outside the eucharist with those who, for a legitimate reason, were unable to be present — especially the sick and dying. Sometimes communion from the reserved sacrament took place even in a liturgical assembly, in a weekday "liturgy of the 'presanctified.'" Communion has also been shared from the reserved sacrament apart from the celebration of the eucharist before, during, and after the Mass. Quite often, even today, the reserved sacrament is used for the communion of the people at Mass; the efforts to prohibit or at least discourage this practice are an indication that church officials consider it less than desirable.

The reason the communion service falls short of the eucharist is that it fails to express the unified shape of eucharistic celebration. The action of placing the gifts becomes clearer in the praise and thanksgiving of the eucharistic prayer. This in turn becomes clearer still in the interaction and interrelationship of communion that is shared in bread and cup. The varied presence of Christ the Priest in his Body, the church, emerges in the dynamic rhythm of the celebration and cannot be limited to one mode of presence — as it is if the eucharistic rhythm is disrupted, muted or absent.

Families may dine for days on the remains of a feast, but it would be unusual to celebrate a special occasion in such a way. What goes into the preparation of a special meal has as much to do with the mood of the occasion as with the food that is placed upon the table (as the movie *Babette's Feast* shows). It is much the same with the gathering of disciples on the Lord's Day. Jesus' disciples do not learn or practice Jesus' manner of table fellowship by receiving communion that derives from a previous celebration or from the celebration of another family of faith. Such a communion may nourish personal devotion, but it will not form the Body of Christ.

Jesus' command to his disciples was "Do this in memory of me" — not say this, look at this, or receive this. The eucharist is first of all an action. It is the action of Jesus in praise and thanksgiving, dedicating himself to the service of all by offering himself to the God who identifies with humanity. It is, at the same time, the action of Christ as church, identifying us with himself in his self-offering as we join in praise and thanksgiving and share his table. In this way, Jesus makes us his Body and shapes us in his image. Redemption means that Jesus' action is worldwide and co-extensive with human life. Nevertheless, that action is ritually or sacramentally present in its fullness only in eucharistic celebration.

The early Christians did not risk death to receive communion but to do the memorial of the Lord's sacrifice on the Lord's Day.[22] Had it been sufficient (or possible) for the priest to offer the sacrifice alone, and had it been enough for them to have communion privately at home, they would not have had to make themselves subject to capital punishment for the crime of gathering to celebrate the eucharist. Christians today learn Jesus' manner of table fellowship and way of life not from books or even the scriptures, nor from sharing a presanctified communion. These things show them to be a collection of students, as in a classroom, and a collection of eaters, as in an airplane at mealtime, not as the fully active community of Jesus' disciples. They are that community only by gathering together, listening to the word, setting the table and preparing the meal, saying the prayer, breaking the bread, sharing the meal and going out to live as Jesus did, as bread for the world.

Consequently, despite the scholastic distinction between sacrament and sacrifice, and the subsequent emphasis on that distinction, sacrament (meal to be shared) and liturgical sacrifice (shared meal) are one and are distinguished only in terms of perspective. But just as intention must lead to action, so ritual continuity is necessary for the meaning of the eucharist to be complete. Thus, although sacramental communion apart from the sacrifice is a sharing in the sacrifice, it is necessarily less and is less effective than the celebration of the sacrifice in its entirety, when the assembly's ritual gestures identify it with Christ. Engaging wholeheartedly in the sacrifice has a dynamic effect that is lacking in simply sharing communion, which may be no more than the expression of private devotion and which certainly leaves the recipients passive and dependent. Engaging in the eucharistic action is what shapes the assembled community as the Body of Christ and commits it to realizing Christ's redemptive presence for the salvation of the world.

This recognition leads to the realization that the encouragement of more frequent communion — evident since the Council of Trent but especially apparent since Pope Pius X — was itself short-sighted and too narrow in its focus. Growing as it did out of medieval devotionalism and sixteenth-century polemicism, it has maintained a clericalism in the proclamation and celebration of the paschal mystery; it has perpetuated the notion that the lay role is passive and dependent, confined to receiving the gifts consecrated by the priest who alone acts *in persona Christi*. Compensating for the defects of the communion service by introducing a prayer of thanksgiving "to replace the regular, official eucharistic prayer of the Mass"[23] leaves the impression that the community is not so much deprived of the eucharist as it is deprived of a priest. Yet a priest — out of sight and perhaps with little or no relationship to the community — has put bread on the community's table, so it is not completely abandoned. The community's "orphaned" and dependent status is highlighted by the suggestion that mention should be made of the community with which the priest-pastor is celebrating the eucharist and that the assembly should be urged to "unite itself in spirit with that community."[24] What this assembly does is then clearly dependent upon and derivative from the action of another assembly, and it is publicly announced as such.

Undoubtedly, the more intense eucharistic experience coming from more frequent communion has been a major factor in the movement to extend the participation of the laity as full members of the Body of Christ. But unfortunately, it has also set up a situation where it is still possible to remain fixated at the level of an objective "real presence" and fail to move on to the reality toward which the sacrament is oriented, toward the unity and mission of the Body of Christ.

As a consequence, the priest's role in the community is restricted to consecrating bread. But more significantly, the community's growth is stifled and it is kept at a level of immaturity at which it does not recognize its identity and mission as the Body of Christ. As long as people remain preoccupied with bread as the Body of Christ, they will not look beyond the bread to see themselves growing to the full stature of Christ as God's work of art.[25]

Historically, as the community was left out of the liturgy, the eucharistic bread became independent of the eucharist, and eucharistic devotions became the means whereby the laity asserted a claim to the otherwise clerical eucharist. In SWAP, a eucharistic devotionalism that hinders growth to maturity is likely to be perpetuated. In SWAP, the sacrificial meal of the eucharist has become a sacrificeless meal, a comfortable meal that fails to challenge or to demand commitment.

Chapter Four Endnotes

1. For places in the document that could lead to this conclusion, see Directory, nos. 12c, 20, 23, 46, 50.

2. The Directory here cites the 1983 letter of the Congregation for the Doctrine of the Faith regarding the minister of the eucharist; see *Origins* 13 (1983): 229–233.

3. Hoyt L. Hickman, "Prayers of Thanksgiving," 125.

4. In addition to Hickman, "Prayers of Thanksgiving," see also F.J. van Beeck, "Praise and Thanksgiving in Noneucharistic Communion Services," *Worship* 60 (1986): 423–434.

5. Only selected points most relevant to our focus will be noted here. For fuller considerations, see David N. Power, *The Sacrifice We Offer: The Tridentine Dogma and Its Reinterpretation* (New York: Crossroad, 1987); Kenneth Stevenson, *Eucharist and Offering* (New York: Pueblo, 1986); Kenneth Stevenson, *Accept This Offering: The Eucharist as Sacrifice Today* (Collegeville: The Liturgical Press, 1989).

6. See, for example, Augustine, *City of God,* 10, 6: "A true sacrifice is every work which is done that we may be united to God in holy fellowship, and which has a reference to that supreme good and end in which alone we can be truly blessed." I have used Marcus Dods' translation in *The City of God* (New York: Modern Library, 1950), 309.

7. Council of Trent, Session 22, "Teaching and canons on the most holy sacrifice of the Mass," especially Chapter 2.

8. SC, no. 47; see also LG, no.11.

9. LG, no. 10.

10. See *Mediator Dei,* nos. 85–95.

11. I have developed in a more detailed way how the assembly is the celebrant of the eucharist and how it is sacramentally transformed through its activity, in *Gathering for Eucharist: A Theology of Sunday Assembly* (Old Hickory, TN: Pastoral Arts Associates, 1982). See especially the conclusions regarding levels of symbolization, pp. 55–60.

12. See Gregory Dix, *The Shape of the Liturgy* (London: Dacre Press, 1945).

13. For further discussion, see my "The Congregation's Share in the Eucharistic Prayer," *Worship* 52 (1978): 329–341, reprinted in R. Kevin Seasoltz, ed., *Living Bread, Saving Cup: Readings on the Eucharist* (Collegeville: The Liturgical Press, 1982), 113–125. For a more detailed consideration of the significance of this, see my "Spirituality of Eucharistic Prayer," *Worship* 58 (1984): 359–372.

14. See Xavier Leon-Dufour, *Sharing the Eucharistic Bread: The Witness of the New Testament* (New York: Paulist Press, 1987), 30.

15. GIRM, no. 283 [DOL 208, no. 1673].

16. For further considerations, see Ralph A. Keifer's excellent analysis, "Preparation of the Altar

and the Gifts, or Offertory?"
Worship 48 (1974): 595–600,
especially 598–600.

17. The spiritualizing of sacrifice,
which began in the Old Testament and continues in the New,
is key to understanding early
Christian sacrificial language; see
Robert J. Daly, *The Origins of the
Christian Docrine of Sacrifice* (Philadelphia: Fortress Press, 1978).

18. See Martin Hengel, The *Atone-
ment: The Origins of the Doctrine
in the New Testament* (Philadelphia:
Fortress Press, 1981); but see also
Sam K. Williams, *Jesus' Death as
Saving Event: The Background and
Origin of a Concept* (Missoula,
MT: Scholars Press, 1975).

19. See Gustav Aulén, *Christus
Victor* (New York: Macmillan,
1969).

20. Frances M. Young, *Sacrifice and
the Death of Christ* (Philadelphia:
Westminster, 1975), 99.

21. Robert Hovda, "It Begins
With the Assembly," in Secretariat
of the Bishops' Committee on
the Liturgy, ed., *The Environment
for Worship* (Washington, D.C.:
United States Catholic Conference,
1980), 38.

22. See Gregory Dix, *The Shape of
the Liturgy,* 153.

23. J. Frank Henderson, "When
Lay People Preside," 110.
Henderson's choice of words,
while unfortunate, is revealing.

24. Directory, no. 42.

25. See Ephesians 2:10, 4:13.

Liturgical Leadership and Ordination

A central theological point at issue concerns the celebrant of the eucharist: Is it the assembled community — the sacrament of the church and the Body of Christ — or is it the priest — the minister of Christ and of the church? According to our tradition, the assembly does not come to participate in the priest's Mass but to do the memorial of the Lord, at which one of its members — the ordained priest — presides.[1] Restoring this tradition to our contemporary experience is crucial to implementing a sound ecclesiology and to facilitating a resolution to the present crisis regarding ordained ministry. Until it is accepted as much in practice as it is in theory that the assembly celebrates the sacraments, the church will be unable to break free of clericalism's hold. Even with the expansion of lay ministries that accompanies the clergy shortage, SWAP will likely increase the problem.

The intensified clericalism that accompanies the clergy shortage and SWAP is apparent in colloquialisms such as "priestless communities," "priestless Sundays" and "priestless Masses." It is also apparent in references to assemblies without priests as assemblies "in expectation of a priest."[2] Such clericalism — the ideology of a privileged caste — is not, as it might seem, a matter of putting too high a value on the priest. It is, rather, an inadequate appreciation of the role that the sacrament of orders plays in the life and worship of the church.

Since a faith community without the eucharist is less able to maintain itself as the Body of Christ, terminology like "priestless Sundays" and "Sunday Worship in the Absence of a Priest" could be taken to imply that the community is dependent upon the priest before it can be the Body of Christ. That is not the case, of course. The action of the Spirit makes and maintains the church as Christ's Body, even if the primary sacramental symbol of that identity is the eucharist (itself the action of the Spirit).

The terminology can be challenged for another reason. Concentrating on the absence of the priest obscures the real loss to the community — not of the priest but of the eucharist. It is the absence of the eucharist that most fundamentally weakens ecclesial communion and impedes the community's — and the church's — continuing transformation into the Body of Christ. The tragedy is not priestless parishes, Sundays or Masses but parishes, Sundays and Sunday worship without the eucharist.

Nevertheless, being priestless does represent a loss to the parish. It indicates that the parish, to some extent, lacks ecclesial reality, and this diminished ecclesial reality has the potential of further weakening the community. A community unable to celebrate the eucharist is unable to realize itself fully as church. Without the nourishment and self-realization that comes from actually celebrating the eucharist, a community of disciples necessarily loses much of the concrete experience of being Christ's Body. Its identification with Christ can become theoretical and verbal rather than experiential and sacramental.

Being priestless of itself also indicates the community's lack of ecclesial reality in relation to the broader church. The fact that the community's actual pastoral leader is not ordained weakens the bonds of ecclesial communion that ordination symbolizes. In light of the history of ordination and the ordination liturgy, the failure to ordain the actual leader of such a community is a denial of full ecclesial communion and a refusal to permit a community to be and become church.[3] The church's ministerial structure is sacramental, not juridical; it is not a matter of conveying certain powers. The ministerial structure has its rationale in the character of the priestly community of the baptized and their participation in the mission of the church. The laying on of hands in ordination is an invocation of the Spirit that constitutes the pastoral leader of a community as a sign of communion in the church. It also enables the celebrations of the local community to be recognized as the sacraments, which are intrinsic and constitutive structural principles of church. Deprivation of this ministry leaves a community on the periphery of church, without the encouragement it needs to enter into the heart of the communion of grace that is church. It is, consequently, a denial of full communion and ecclesiality.

Canonically, of course, a priest is the pastor, even if that priest only visits occasionally and is not involved in the community's life. It is on this basis that the claim is made that no parish community is "priestless." Were the claim based on the theological facts that Christ is the one Priest and that Christ is indeed present where two or three gather in faith, it would be more convincing. The pastoral fact is that the persons who actually function as pastors of communities without priests — whether called pastors or not — are not ordained; and this says something about the ecclesial reality of such communities.

The crucial issue, then, is the ecclesial character of the community whose actual (if not canonical) leaders and pastors are not ordained. To explore this issue requires considering the significance of ordination for liturgical and pastoral leadership, the situation of pastors who are not ordained, and the relationship of the priest and the church.

The Significance of Pastoral Ordination[4]

In the first centuries of Christianity, there was no problem of assemblies without presiders: The one who presided at the eucharist was the same one who presided over the Christian community — the bishop. Evidence suggests that in the bishop's absence, provision was made for someone else to preside as a delegate, usually a presbyter or deacon. However, even though leadership in the community — and consequently at its eucharist — was an acknowledged ministry, community leaders were not thought of as constituting a distinct clerical class until the third century. Even then, pastoral leadership and liturgical leadership remained correlated for centuries.[5]

Though ministry is an intrinsic and constitutive element of church, studies of scripture, history and theology clearly show that Jesus drew no blueprints for the shape and character of that ministry. It has evolved, and will continue to evolve, in response to the church's pastoral needs and its mission in the world. The New Testament, for example, says nothing about the requirements for presiding at the eucharist. In the gospels, Jesus presides at the feeding of the multitudes, at the breaking of the bread at the Last Supper and at the meals after the resurrection. Acts speaks of Paul presiding at the breaking of the bread in two instances (20:7 – 15; 27:35), and Paul himself refers to it in 1 Corinthians 10:16. Beyond that, nothing is said about requirements or qualifications. The first Christians undoubtedly followed traditional Jewish practice, which provided for the orderly fulfillment of responsibilities in synagogue and domestic worship. Competency — the ability to pray publicly and to lead others in prayer — and function within the community — a leadership role — were determining factors. Temple worship, which required hereditary cultic priests functioning in consecrated territory according to prescribed rules, was irrelevant.

The New Testament documents ignore the question of qualifications for presiding because of the uniqueness of Christian worship. The *whole* of Christian existence was caught up into a "cultic" context.[6] Refusing to divide life into separate spheres of sacred and secular (as the Temple hierarchy had), Jesus and his later followers saw all of life as the worship of God. As a consequence, even the eucharist was essentially an act of evangelic proclamation,[7] and liturgical leadership was a prophetic role.[8]

The community's leaders, particularly the patrons of the house churches, probably functioned as liturgical leaders if they had the charism for it. If not, they probably had some say in who did. Church founders sometimes appointed the leaders with prayer and fasting (Acts 14:23). At other times, the leaders seem to have emerged or to have been selected on the basis of charism or ability (e.g., 1 Corinthians 12:28). Eventually, appointment to office won out over selection based on having the charism the office entailed. Yet, though contemporary Judaism did regulate liturgical leadership, there is little evidence for ordination rites in the first century in either Judaism or Christianity.[9] By the early second century, some form of ordination for pastoral leaders may have existed in some areas, especially the Asia Minor of Ignatius of Antioch. But who, if anyone, did the ordaining is unclear. 1 Timothy 4:14 speaks of presbyters ordaining; in 2 Timothy 1:6 it is "Paul" who ordains. This may indicate the coexistence of distinct polities: a collegial presbyterate (1 Timothy) and a mono-episcopate, that is, a bishop alone (2 Timothy).

By the end of the second century a clear ministerial structure founded on some form of mono-episcopate appears to have become standard. However, not until the third century do we have clear evidence of a ritual of installation or of ordination. In our earliest ordination ritual, in Hippolytus' *Apostolic Tradition* (c. 215), the community, the presbytery and bishops from neighboring communities are all involved in ordaining a bishop, with one of the latter requested to take a leading role in the laying on of hands and the prayers (2–3). The bishop ordains the presbyter, with the assistance of the other presbyters (7), but the bishop alone ordains the deacon (8).[10] (Interestingly, modern rites for appointing or commissioning ministers — clearly distinguished theologically from ordination — have the same basic ritual structure as the ancient ordination rites!) All ordinations seem to take place with the community's consent, or at least in its presence, and in the context of the celebration of the word and the eucharist.

The significance of pastoral ordination is thus clear in Hippolytus: "Ordination is for the clergy, on account of their liturgical duties."[11] Gordon Lathrop captures the sense well when he says that "the leadership of the liturgy is part of the liturgy."[12] A liturgical initiation into the role is the appropriate way to begin it.

By this point, episcopal and presbyteral ministries were interpreted as being priestly, and leadership in the liturgy was becoming the basis for extra-liturgical leadership in the church, even though eucharistic presidency was still the liturgical expression of pastoral responsibility. Yet, for Hippolytus, the bishop is the high priest of a priestly assembly, not a person with the power of offering and consecrating. Ordination is the act of God and of the community by which the ordained is strengthened for ministry and supported with the acceptance and prayer of the community. There is no evidence that Hippolytus or his contemporaries regarded it as the conferral of sacred powers; nor is there any reference to the presbyter as the one who consecrates and offers sacrifice. (A curiosity of history is that Pope Leo XIII in 1896 ruled Anglican orders invalid on the basis of defect of form — due to the Anglican elimination from the medieval rites of any references to the power to consecrate and to offer sacrifice — and defect of intention — due to the positive exclusion of the will to confer the power to consecrate and to offer sacrifice.)

Emerging at this period is the idea that the presider acts in the place of Christ, the High Priest, who is present in the assembly. The understanding we find in Cyprian may be regarded as typical.[13] The imitation of Christ is the essential vocation of every Christian; imitating Christ brings about the presence and activity of Christ. Liturgical rites show that Christian living is such imitation. However, the leader of the eucharist makes Christ present — is a type of Christ — in a special way, by imaging the unity of mutual love that Christ brought about by his *passio* (death and resurrection). Thus, not only the bishop's Christian identity but also the church's identity depends on his imitation of Christ to express and maintain ecclesial communion.

To be effective leaders, then, bishops and presbyters must imitate Christ in their lives by fostering communion. And eucharistic presidency is the deepest expression of this.

> For if Christ Jesus, our Lord and God, is himself the great High Priest of God the Father and if he offered himself as a sacrifice to the Father and directed that this should be done in remembrance of him, then without a doubt that priest truly serves in Christ's place who imitates what Christ did and he offers up a true and complete sacrifice to God the Father in the church when he proceeds to offer it just as he sees Christ himself to have offered it.[14]

Thus, for Cyprian,

> the leader of the eucharist becomes [a] vehicle for the presence of Christ in the liturgical assembly to the degree that the church by its faith is able to perceive in his actions, as manifestations of his person, the leadership of Christ the priest in the sacrificial events of his life, death, and resurrection.[15]

There is no indication that the bishop was regarded as having received cultic powers handed down from Christ; his liturgical role was because of his pastoral role. Even earlier, the bishop-presider had functioned as the community's focus of unity. Ignatius' argument for the office of bishop was that only a single leader could hold an easily divided community together.[16] Public election and ordination guaranteed at least an initial popular support. But the bishop was not only the focus of unity for the local church. The fact that the bishops of neighboring churches (usually at least three, a custom that the Council of Nicaea made mandatory) had to ratify the election and do the ordaining showed that the new bishop was accepted within the wider network or communion of churches as one who was able to maintain and promote the unity of the broader church. Thus, the bishop-presider symbolized and ensured unity between his local church and the catholic church. He was the sacramental focus of unity both locally and ecumenically, either in his own person or, analogously, in the person of his delegate.

Liturgical leadership was gradually confined to the ordained, though others probably shared in preaching and public prayer for some time. There was a movement from charism — the ability to function — to office — being formally entrusted with a role. Liturgical functions were clericalized. There was a shift from corporate presidency to individual presidency. By the end of the fourth century it was apparently unthinkable for anyone other than a priest (bishop or presbyter) to preside at the eucharist and lead the eucharistic prayer.[17] Though there is a long tradition of "extraordinary" or "special" ministers in other sacraments, there are, as we have seen, few historical instances of this in the case of eucharistic presidency. Subsequent to the Carolingian reformation, all liturgical leadership was effectively restricted to the ordained. In time, celebrations of the eucharist not presided over by a presbyter or a bishop were prohibited and judged invalid.[18]

Though liturgical leadership was never unregulated, how that role was conceived had undergone significant change by the end of the Carolingian era. Previously, the liturgy had been regarded as the prayer of Christ, with the church associated with that prayer through the Spirit. Ministry was regarded as the gift of the Spirit working in and through the community of faith. The Carolingian era came to see the liturgy as the work of the priest, who acted as the instrument of Christ, independent of the assembly's prayer, and as the one on whom the faithful depended. (The differences here may be based on two different images of Christ's mediatorship: the image of Christ as the eternal high priest who intercedes with the Father versus the image of Christ as the one who distributes grace.[19]) Accordingly, ordination came to be regarded as the conferral of the power to act in the person of Christ and, especially, to "confect" the eucharist. Priestly ministry was essentially cultic rather than pastoral.

As a consequence of ordination, the individual was independent of the community and yet acted, even in private, as the public minister of the church, e.g., in reconciling sinners and in offering Mass. Absolute ordination — ordination without reference to a community and a role of pastoral leadership — is closely connected with the development of private penance and the private Mass, all of which came about in the Carolingian era.

Absolute ordination, because it creates a priest without a clear relationship to an actual community, is tangentially relevant to our considerations. The medieval benefices and the later canonical notion that the diocesan priest is ordained "for the bishop's table" *(ad mensam episcopi)* did maintain some relationship to a community — in the latter case, to the diocesan community. However, the fact that a priest without a community is conceivable means that a community without a priest is also conceivable. Nevertheless, although present church regulations permit a priest to celebrate the eucharist without a community — the private Mass — a community cannot celebrate the eucharist without a priest.

The earlier understanding was that the one who leads the community presides at its worship. That person was ordained in communion with the presbyterate headed by the bishop. A bishop presided at the ordination as the sign of the unity of the local church and its union with other ecclesial communities and local churches. The ordained presbyter functioned through relationship to the community and to the bishop. He was a sacrament of the assembly's unity. By making the bishop somehow present in the local community[20] — or, better, by being a sign of communion with the bishop — he was a sacrament of its union with the wider church. The presbyter was not merely a figure representing an external authority, or an individual exercising a power inaccessible to others: He was the member of the community who led its worship. All pastoral leadership was regarded as a matter of coordinating and integrating the faith, life and worship of the local community.

As the pastoral leader and minister to the community, the priest in the liturgy sacramentalized Christ presiding as the head of his Body, the church. But the priest's presiding role was because the priest was the member of the church who had the responsibility to ensure that the assembly celebrated the Lord's Supper. The priest did this by sacramentalizing the common union of this community with Christ, the inward source of its life, and its union with other communities in the local church. Then, through the bishop — the chief liturgist of the local church and head of the presbyterate — the presiding presbyter sacramentalized the common union of the local church with the whole body of local churches, not only as they existed currently but in their communion over time.

The dominant interpretation since the early scholastic period in the high middle ages has been that the priest, at ordination, receives powers that were first given to the apostles at the Last Supper and then transmitted through the centuries by ordination so that the priest might act *in persona Christi*. The power to "confect" the eucharist (that is, to change bread and wine into the Body and Blood of Christ) is one that the priest has by virtue of ordination. It is, in fact, his highest power. (This accounts for the scholastic reluctance to see the episcopacy as sacramentally distinct from the presbyterate, since bishops and priests have this power equally. Thus, in scholastic terminology, presbyters are ordained, bishops merely conse-crated.) The priest may exercise this power without reference to a community and its pastoral needs, although the bishop may restrict its public use. The priest may even exercise this power privately, without the presence of members of the com-munity. Though Aquinas and others regarded the priest as the instrument of Christ (who actually makes the eucharist), the tendency has been to see this as a personal power of the priest.

This approach to priesthood and the eucharist — sometimes caricatured as a "relay race" or a "pipeline" approach — has been called into question not only by research into scriptural and historical sources, but also by the magisterial teaching of Vatican II. The "power" approach has no scriptural base, nor is there much that can be cited as evidence for it in the early centuries. We find no evidence of ordination until the end of the first and the beginning of the second century, and no clear statement until the early third century. Vatican II situates the priest's liturgical role within a pastoral, rather than a "power" or cultic, context.

The "power" approach to ordained ministry is largely the consequence of the influence of feudal culture and is not prevalent until the Carolingian era, which emphasized, for example, the power of the keys. Scholastic theologians first distinguished the power of order *(potestas ordinis)* and the power of jurisdiction *(potestas iurisdictionis)*. They then distinguished between power over the *eucharistic* Body of Christ (power of order) and power over the *ecclesial* Body of Christ (power of jurisdiction). "Power" and "eucharist" were generally corre-lated terms, with the hierarchy ranked by their relationship to the eucharist.[21] Scholastic theologians presupposed a heavily cultic notion of ordained ministry and gave little attention to relating a pastoral role to the eucharist. The clericalization of monasteries, where previously priests had been barely toler-ated, is another expression of the developing cultic under-standing of ordained ministry, since priest-monks rarely had pastoral responsibilities.

Vatican II, following scriptural and historical studies, reclaimed the ancient position.[22] It set aside the cultic view, which cor-related power and the eucharist, in favor of a view that rooted the priest's liturgical leadership in pastoral leadership. The whole community is a priestly people, a sacrament of Christ. Such a sacramental community needs no mediator other than Christ. Thus, Christ the Priest is present when a community gathers in his name (Matthew 18:20). Christ is present to them immediately in the Spirit, with his presence realized sacramentally and celebrated by the whole church in its life and worship. A collegial sacramental ministry is then responsible for safeguarding the community's sacramentality and priesthood. This is liturgically expressed in the priest's role as the presider in the worshiping assembly.

While the cultic approach — with its emphasis on unique powers — is still in evidence,[23] it does not harmonize well with the approach to priesthood taken at Vatican II. The cultic approach is, first of all, too narrow. It fails to recognize the evangelical and prophetic — hence, pastoral and communal — character of the sacraments, which are the acts of the Spirit enlivening the church. Second, its emphasis on ontological modifications within the person ordained regards sacramental powers as an individualistic possession. It gives too little attention to the concept of communion — the collegial nature of the priesthood and the relationship of presbyters to the bishop. Third, it fails to respect the function and the communal and sacramental nature of both the ordained ministry and the community as a whole. While the universal priesthood of the faithful differs from the ordained priesthood of the clergy in essence and not simply degree,[24] the ordained priesthood is a ministry — and hence a sacrament — in, of, and to the community; it is not a higher status.

The "power of orders" understanding of priestly ministry was a credible and convincing one within a particular socio-cultural context using a particular philosophical approach. But in our time there is the risk that this approach will appear magical and unreal and will inadequately communicate the true nature and function of pastoral ordination: relationship to and in community and relationship to the eucharist and eucharistic ministry.

This does not mean that eucharistic presidency is "up for grabs," as though anyone could legitimately preside at the eucharist. There is no evidence that this was ever accepted practice. The reason is not that "anyone" lacks the power the priest has.

It is, rather, that the church is an organic and organized body not confined to a local community or to a particular time; that the church requires a stable ministry recognizable as such; and that liturgical leadership is normally to be correlated with pastoral leadership by authorized ministers who are accepted by the community and by the broader church to speak in its name. From an ecclesial perspective, the priest symbolizes the unity of the assembly, its communion with the bishop and its communion with the whole church; it is because of this that the priest, at the same time, symbolizes Christ to the community gathered for the eucharist. Priests do this in the eucharist precisely because they do it in the community.

Thus, the fact that the priest functions "in the person of Christ" means that the priest functions as a *sacramental representation,* not as a substitute or stand-in for Christ. It is still Christ who is the Head of his Body; it is still Christ who presides and whose prayer is the prayer of the church. The priest represents Christ on the level of liturgical and sacramental reality, not on the level of theological reality, and does so in two correlative ways: by exercising a ministry of leadership to build the church as the Body of Christ and by leading the community in the prayer of Christ.[25] But it is the assembled church, not the priest, that celebrates the sacraments and is the fullest sacramental representation of Christ.

While the ordained priest does sacramentally represent both the church and Christ, the priest does not do so in the liturgy as a cultic person — because of "powers" received — but as a pastoral person — as one in pastoral leadership. Ordained for this ministry, the priest imitates Christ by fostering the communion, the unity of mutual love, established by the paschal mystery.

There is a liturgy of ordination not because the person ordained needs certain "powers" but because the person ordained is to lead the liturgy. Leadership at liturgy is a powerful human symbol; the leader of the liturgy necessarily takes on something of the effective nature of the liturgy itself and becomes personally a liturgical symbol — a risky business indeed, both for the leader and for the community. The leader may bear no more resemblance to Christ than does bread, but the power of the Spirit shows forth Christ. It is for this reason that a Spirit-invoking liturgy of ordination exists; prayers for the Spirit are needed for such a leader and for the community. All of this means that the ordained priest, then, exists not to exercise "powers" but for the benefit of the assembly, which needs the ministry of leadership.[26]

That the priest acts "in the person of Christ," when interpreted primarily from a cultic understanding of priesthood, has been used as the basis for arguing that the priest must be male (to image Christ, who was male, there must be a "natural resemblance"[27]) and celibate (to image Christ, who was unmarried and is bridegroom of the church[28]). But in presiding, particularly in leading the eucharistic prayer, the priest speaks in the name of the assembly and the church whose prayer is the prayer of Christ. The priest's role of representing Christ is thus inseparable from his role of representing the church. The two roles are enacted simultaneously, even if on the level of liturgical experience the ecclesial role appears primary.

The simultaneous enactment of the two roles and their relationship are evident in the liturgy. The pattern of eucharistic prayer found in the Roman Canon and other texts is that the priest prays in the name of the assembled church, the Body of Christ; that is, the priest prays in the first person plural. References to Christ are in the third person. At no point does the priest pray in the name of Christ (in the first person singular). Christ's words at the Last Supper are cited, but they are in the context of a narrative addressed by the church to God, and this narrative *(Qui pridie)* continues an invocation *(Quam oblationem)* offered in the name of the church. Thus, the priest's role of representing Christ is the consequence of his role of representing the church, the Body of Christ.

Where the present situation stands in sharp contrast to that of the first centuries is that in some communities today, liturgical and pastoral leadership are not combined in the same person. Instead, the liturgical leader is an ordained outsider, and the pastoral leader, not ordained, is unable to exercise liturgical leadership in the eucharistic assembly.

Pastors Who Are Not Ordained

At certain points, the Roman *Directory* seems somewhat defensive or unsure of itself. This is especially the case when it speaks of the priest, whether directly (as in a discussion of the assembly's relationship to the priest and to its lay leader) or indirectly (as when it speaks of the eucharistic sacrifice and the assembly's share in it). It prefers to speak of assemblies "in expectation of a priest" rather than "without a priest" or "in the absence of a priest" (27). Yet it does not seem comfortable in speaking of either the relationship between the priest and the community or of an assembly without a priest. Emphasis that the lay leader acts as "one among equals" (39) suggests that the priest is regarded as superior to the laity in the areas of liturgy and pastoral care, exercising a priesthood that merely differs in degree from the common priesthood of the faithful. It also implies that the lay leader's only ministry is a "suppletory" liturgical office (31) that does not, for example, include preaching a homily (43).[29] The *Directory* seems reluctant to see the lay worship-leader as a minister or as one who is exercising a ministry. In addition, it totally ignores the role of the lay worship-leader in the community's life, perhaps assuming that the lay worship-leader has no pastoral role.

The issue of SWAP will become increasingly problematic as lay administrators (pastors in fact if not in name) take on more roles that traditionally have been reserved for the ordained priest. In many communities, they are already administering parishes and their programs, supervising the process of initiation and coordinating parish ministries and all that pertains to the life and mission of the faith community. They are baptizing, marrying, burying and leading Sunday worship. There are no theological or historical reasons why they cannot be authorized to anoint the sick.[30] There is ample precedent for them to hear confessions,[31] and many actually do. The only "powers" that are refused them are presiding in absolving sinners and celebrating the eucharist.

There are, it seems, two conflicting and not easily reconciled theologies of priesthood in the contemporary church. One theology, officially espoused at Vatican II, gives primacy to the pastoral role of bishops and priests: Bishops and priests are

120

pastors, and their sacramental role flows from their role as pastors. Logically, according to this theology, all those who serve as pastors should be ordained to exercise the appropriate sacramental roles: Apart from the sacramental role, they function as do priest pastors, even to the point of providing a link with the broader church.

The other theology, a holdover from the past, regards priests as cultic functionaries (with the power of orders) who may incidentally have a pastoral role (with the power of jurisdiction). Lay pastors are distinguished from priest pastors only by the fact that lay pastors lack the power to preside at the eucharist and at reconciliation. They are denied ordination — prescinding from the issue of women's ordination — because they are not celibate.

Admittedly, the two mutually inconsistent theologies can both be found in the compromise documents of Vatican II. The first, however, clearly has priority in those documents. The second enters in at points, but is never fundamental. In subsequent ecclesiastical documents, however, this "power of orders" or cultic theology has again been emphasized, and, as an expression of clericalism, it is at the root of a dilemma.

The dilemma is this:[32] Lay pastors in priestless parishes are denied ordination but are distinguished from priests only by the fact that they may not preside at the eucharist, at reconciliation and at anointing. Does this mean that the pastoral functions of lay pastors are not sacramental and priestly and, consequently, that the only sacramental and priestly functions that a priest has are presiding at these sacraments? Or, if we reject this cultic-functionary view of ministerial priesthood as untenable in the light of history and Vatican II, why do we not admit that the commissioning of lay pastors to an office more significant than the diaconate is — or can be — sacramental?[33] In that case, why do we deny lay pastors the sacramental presiding roles that flow from and express their already established pastoral roles as leaders of the faith community and as links with the broader church? There seems to be a theological inconsistency: Lay pastors have the priestly *pastoral* role but not the priestly *sacramental* role that historically and theologically flows from it.

My point is not to argue that lay pastors can preside at the eucharist and at reconciliation or that they should assume this role. It is to indicate that there is a theological inconsistency in the present situation regarding ministry and that it has ramifications for ecclesiology.

That the pastoral leaders of communities are not ordained is not unsettling because they consequently lack the "power to confect" the sacraments of eucharist and reconciliation. Rather, the denial of ordination logically operates as a refusal to recognize pastoral leaders as fully competent ministers; a refusal to recognize the communities that they lead as being capable of celebrating the eucharist; and, thereby, a refusal to recognize these communities as "church" in the full sense. The implication is that such local communities are lacking in ecclesial reality. Men are ordained who will have little, if any, pastoral relationship to communities; but ministers who actually serve as pastors are denied ordination.

Just as SWAP replaces the eucharist, perfect contrition — possibly within a penitential celebration — replaces the sacrament of reconciliation *even if* a priest is available but there are not enough priests present to hear individual confessions. Thus, the restriction that only a priest can preside at the eucharist and at reconciliation leads to parallel and similar liturgical substitutes for these sacraments when no priest is available. The individualistic and devotional character of the substitute for sacramental reconciliation, even when it takes place in common, strengthens the suspicion that SWAP can easily move in the direction of becoming similarly devotional.

Taking into account both the substitute ministries and substitute liturgies that are provided, it is no surprise that not celebrating the eucharist weakens the local community's bonds of communion with the broader church. It also debilitates the community's self-realization as church. The community is not simply *unable* to celebrate the eucharist; it is, in fact, *prevented* from doing so by the broader church that refuses to recognize through ordination the legitimacy of the community's pastoral ministry. Furthermore, the broader church fails to recognize the community's full ecclesiality through eucharistic celebration. The "language" of ordination speaks sacramentally of the unified and unitive life of the church.[34] It does so through the individuals whom it constitutes as signs of the bonds of communion in the local community and with the broader church. By refusing to fully recognize the pastoral leaders of such communities, the church denies full ecclesial status.

Gathered in Steadfast Faith, unlike the *Directory,* emphasizes responsibility for mission[35] and stresses that the assembly is a focus for broader life and ministry.[36] In addition, it details the qualifications for those who would serve as liturgical leaders. These are worth citing in full because, apart from the additional requirements of male gender and commitment to celibacy, they seem indistinguishable from the qualifications for candidates for ordination:

> Those chosen for this ministry should not merely be "volunteers," but persons who exhibit a living appreciation for scripture; a deep reverence for the eucharist; an active prayer life; an exemplary moral life; a spirit of cooperation with the laity and clergy of the particular community; an acceptance by the members of the community; an active involvement in the pastoral life of the community; and both a strong desire and ability to foster participation by lay people as members of the worshiping assembly and in other liturgical roles. . . .
>
> Moreover, the candidates should demonstrate the necessary skills for public speaking that will enable them to be heard and understood in a liturgical setting, as well as the requisite sense of presence that is called for in movement and gesture in prayer. Finally, there should be evidence of the persons' commitment to this ministry, of their availability to exercise it, and of their willingness and ability to integrate within a solid spirituality the exercise of this ministry with personal and family obligations.[37]

The separation of pastoral and liturgical leadership primarily impacts ecclesial communion: It weakens the local community, and it diminishes the local community's relationship to the broader church. However, it also threatens the character of ministry as well. It demoralizes the pastoral minister who is not considered "worthy" of ordination — whether because of marital responsibilities or gender or other factors — even when that minister consciously chooses not to seek ordination. It calls into question the reality of that individual's ministry in the local community because she or he is not fully accredited as a minister of the church able to lead the community in the eucharist as well as in its pastoral life.

Priest and Church

The separation of pastoral and liturgical leadership also demoralizes the priest and threatens the identity of the ordained priest and the character of priestly ministry. This was the special concern voiced in a report adopted in April 1991 by the National Federation of Priests' Councils. The report not only called attention to issues of theology and discipline but also to the effect of priestless parishes on the relationship between priests and parishioners. "In every case when there is a priestless parish there is: a change in the relationship of priest to his people and to his ministry; a change in the experience of the celebration of eucharist by the parishioners; a shift in the people's perception of the identity of the priest."[38]

As individual priests become responsible for sacramental ministry in multiple and geographically separated communities, they necessarily will be removed from the context of a pastoral relationship to the parishioners; such priests lack the day-to-day involvement in the lives of the parish members. For most priests, who committed to priestly ministry because of a call to such pastoral involvement, this is demoralizing because it is depersonalizing. And it is a return to a cultic view of priesthood with a vengeance that tears the heart out of priestly ministry. In addition, the attempt to respond pastorally to the diverse needs of people in multiple parishes can lead quickly to burn-out. If the thrust of ordination is not to convey sacramental powers but to empower the priest as a focus of unity, a priest without a pastoral relationship to a community is an anomaly.

Anti-clericalism is a real danger in such parishes. It can arise as the consequence of anger that the parish has no resident priest. It can be the result of the high status ascribed to the sacramental minister. It can grow out of resentment that the parish and its pastoral leader must accommodate themselves to the priest on the occasions when one is available. Whatever the dynamics, the likelihood is not that priests will be more highly valued because of their scarcity, but rather that they will be devalued and even perhaps regarded as dispensable.

The present situation is likely to become worse. While seminary enrollment figures appear to be stabilizing or slightly increasing in industrialized nations, the number of seminarians and ordinations is not sufficient to balance the number of clergy lost through death, retirement or resignation. And nowhere is the number of candidates for ordination growing in proportion to the growth of the Catholic population. The large number of recruits in developing nations and Eastern Europe is likely to fall as living standards rise, if past U.S. experience holds true.[39] If, as has been claimed, a major obstacle to recruiting seminarians is the failure of priests to actively do so, along with their failure to project an image of satisfaction and fulfillment, how much more is this likely to be the case if priests have sacramental responsibilities in several communities and lay ministers are the practitioners of pastoral ministry?

What is curious is that the individual ordained priest is regarded as capable of being church alone and celebrating the eucharist alone, while the Body of Christ in some locales is unable to realize its identity through eucharistic celebration because its leader in liturgy and in pastoral work is not ordained. While whole communities may not celebrate the eucharist together in order to maintain their public life, individual priests may celebrate the eucharist alone for the sake of private devotion or for the stipend.

The private Mass and SWAP are at opposite poles, equidistant from the eucharist. The origins of the private Mass are understandable in context, even if interpretations conflict.[40] What is less understandable, in light of the character of the eucharist, is that both the private Mass and SWAP are tolerated, while the eucharist is denied to communities.

The Mass celebrated by the priest alone *(missa solitaria)* is a holdover from the obsolete view that the priest alone celebrates the eucharist because of powers available to no one else. Because the priest represents Christ, he may act alone, without a community. Because he represents Christ, he represents the church, and so the church *is* present — even if no one is there. For this reason, the private Mass is considered a public act. So it is argued.

A basic principle of reform stated at Vatican II ruled out such individual and private celebrations.[41] A pragmatic reason for the restoration of concelebration was to eliminate the practice of multiple private celebrations in religious communities and at priests' gatherings. The *General Instruction of the Roman Missal* retreated somewhat, stating that the Mass should not be celebrated by the priest alone "except out of serious necessity."[42] The 1983 Code of Canon Law, promulgated by Pope John Paul II, seemingly returns the matter to the clerical and Counter-Reformation *status quo ante,* saying that the Mass should not be celebrated privately "except for some legitimate and reasonable cause."[43]

However, John Paul II has stated frequently that the Council is the context for interpreting the law.[44] Considering the importance given communal celebration in the *Constitution on the Sacred Liturgy,* neither personal devotion nor the stipend is sufficient to compensate, legitimately and reasonably, for the absence of the community. More precisely, neither private devotion nor the stipend is a legitimate and reasonable justification for the individual priest's refusal to be in community when that is possible. Because the eucharist is an ecclesial event, the priest presiding alone when community celebration is possible violates what he is called to embody. The priest has no more right to the eucharist than a community has, nor should the priest reasonably convert to personal use what is intrinsically social.

In addition to the continuing toleration of the private Mass, the practice of Mass stipends shows that the power-based understanding of ordination is still officially maintained. The rationale for the Mass stipend has generally been developed in terms of the "fruits" of the Mass — the notion of benefits derived from the celebration that are at least partially controlled by the ordained presider.[45] This too depends upon the "power" approach to priesthood. The parallel assumption regarding lay presiders at SWAP is, presumably, either that their role accomplishes nothing or that SWAP is nothing, since church law does not mention their right to a stipend.

Both the private Mass and SWAP contradict what the eucharist says about being church. Both stand in opposition to the clear statement of Vatican II: "No Christian community can be built without roots and foundations in the celebration of the most holy eucharist, and from this all education in the sense of community must begin."[46]

To deny the eucharist to a community is to deny it full ecclesiality. Both denials are implied in the inability or refusal to provide a community with an ordained pastoral leader. To do so is a threat to ministry, both ordained and lay. It is also a threat to the local community. And it is a threat to the church and to the identity and mission of Catholic Christianity, which rest solidly upon sacramental foundations.

Chapter Five
Endnotes

1. Though not clear in recent experience, the role of the assembly as the celebrant of the liturgy and of the sacraments is clear in the early liturgical tradition and in contemporary liturgical theology. It is also presupposed in the current official liturgical books. See Alessandro Pistoia, "L'assemblea come soggetto della celebrazione: Una verifica sui 'Praenotanda' e sui modelli celebrativi dei nuovi libri liturgici," in *Ecclesiologia e Liturgia,* Atti della X Settimana di studio dell'Associazione Professori di Liturgia; Bologna: 28 agosto – 1 settembre 1981 (Casale Monferrato: Casa Editrice Marietti, 1982), 90 – 126.

2. Directory, no. 27.

3. See, for example, Hans-Joachim Schulz, "Die Grundstruktur des kirchlichen Amtes im Spiegel der Eucharistiefeier und der Ordinationsliturgie des römischen und des byzantinischen Ritus," *Catholica* 29 (1975): 325 – 340; Albert Houssiau, "The Theological Significance of the New Ordination Rite," *Louvain Studies* 3 (1970): 31 – 40.

4. For historical and theological surveys, see Paul Bernier, *Ministry in the Church: A Historical and Pastoral Approach* (Mystic, CT: Twenty-Third Publications, 1992); Bernard Cooke, *Ministry to Word and Sacraments: History and Theology* (Philadelphia: Fortress Press, 1976); Nathan Mitchell, *Mission and Ministry: History and Theology in the Sacrament of Order* (Wilmington, DE: Michael Glazier, 1982);

Kenan Osborne, *Priesthood: A History of the Ordained Ministry in the Roman Catholic Church* (New York: Paulist Press, 1988).

5. See especially Edward Schillebeeckx, *Ministry* (New York: Crossroad, 1981) and *The Church with a Human Face: A New and Expanded Theology of Ministry* (New York: Crossroad, 1985).

6. Bernard Cooke, *Ministry to Word and Sacraments,* 528.

7. *Ibid.,* 529.

8. *Ibid.,* 530.

9. See especially Lawrence A. Hoffman, "Jewish Ordination on the Eve of Christianity" in Wiebe Vos and Geoffrey Wainwright, eds., *Ordination Rites: Papers Read at the 1979 Congress of Societas Liturgica* (Rotterdam: Liturgical Ecumenical Center Trust, 1980), 11 – 41; Edward J. Kilmartin, "Ministry and Ordination in Early Christianity against a Jewish Background" in *Ordination Rites,* 42 – 69.

10. Other texts and commentaries may be found in Paul F. Bradshaw, *Ordination Rites of the Ancient Churches of East and West* (New York: Pueblo, 1990) and H. B. Porter, Jr., *The Ordination Prayers of the Ancient Western Churches,* Alcuin Club Collections, No. 49 (London: S.P.C.K., 1967).

11. *Apostolic Tradition,* no. 10.

12. Gordon W. Lathrop, *Holy Things: A Liturgical Theology* (Minneapolis: Fortress Press, 1993), 190.

13. See John D. Laurance, *'Priest' as Type of Christ: The Leader of the Eucharist in Salvation History according to Cyprian of Carthage* (New York: Peter Lang, 1984).

14. Ep. 63, 14, 4. I have used the translation found in G. W. Clarke, trans. and ed., *Ancient Christian Writers,* v. 46, *The Letters of St. Cyprian of Carthage,* v. 3 (New York: Newman Press, 1986), 106.

15. John D. Laurance, *'Priest' as Type of Christ,* 230.

16. See his letter to the Magnesians 7, 1; to the Trallians 2, 2; to the Philadelphians 7, 2.

17. For a study of the development, see Paul Bradshaw, *Liturgical Presidency in the Early Church,* Grove Liturgical Study, No. 36 (Bramcote, Nottingham: Grove Books, 1983).

18. See Innocent III (DS 794), Lateran IV (DS 802), Clement VIII (DS 1084), and especially the 1983 letter of the Congregation of the Faith, "Letter to Bishops on Certain Questions Concerning the Minister of the Eucharist," *Origins* 13 (1983): 229–233.

19. David N. Power, *The Sacrifice We Offer,* 172–173.

20. LG, no. 28; Vatican II, *Decree on the Ministry and Life of Priests (Presbyterorum ordinis)* [hereafter PO], (December 7, 1965), no. 5.

21. Paul Bernier, *Ministry in the Church,* 136.

22. For recent magisterial statements and contemporary theological reflection, see Daniel Donovan, *What Are They Saying About the Ministerial Priesthood?* (New York: Paulist Press, 1992.)

23. The cultic approach is especially used to establish the need for a validly ordained priest to preside at a eucharist if the church is to recognize that celebration as valid. It is often assumed in discussing the admission of women to orders and the ordination of married people.

24. LG, no. 10.

25. Edward J. Kilmartin, *Christian Liturgy: Theology and Practice,* v. 1: *Theology* (Kansas City: Sheed and Ward, 1988), 196.

26. "The fundamental reason why every liturgical celebration needs someone to preside is that no celebrating assembly can exist except in the name of Christ and called together by Christ, rooted in the living tradition of the catholic and apostolic faith." *Leading the Prayer of God's People: Liturgical Presiding for Priests and Laity,* Document of the Association of National Liturgy Secretaries of Europe (Dublin: Columba Press, 1991), 11; reprinted in *National Bulletin on Liturgy* 27 (Fall 1993): 145.

27. Congregation for the Doctrine of the Faith, *Declaration on the Question of the Admission of Women to the Ministerial Priesthood (Inter insigniores)* (October 15, 1976), no. 27. However, the Declaration makes no use of liturgical texts in its argumentation on a sacramental and liturgical question. It simply states that the priest represents Christ as head and shepherd of the church in pronouncing the words of consecration and that this is distinct from, and the basis of, the priest representing the church in

presiding. No liturgical text makes this assumption or this distinction.

28. See Archbishop J. Francis Stafford, "Eucharistic Foundation of Sacerdotal Celibacy," *Origins* 23 (September 2, 1993): 211–216. Stafford argues that there is an incongruity between exercising this role of headship—an exclusive dedication to the bride of Christ as a nuptial union, expressed in offering the sacrifice that is the covenant between Christ and the church—and exercising sexual marriage rights that continue to institute the marital covenant. The priest's "nuptial meaning" (sacramental masculinity) is exercised *in persona Christi* and there is no remaining nuptial meaning in his own person that could be sacramentally expressed in marriage. Any expression of the priest's nuptiality apart from offering the eucharistic sacrifice is adultery. Stafford admits the difficulty of understanding the fact that there are exceptions (e.g., permitting laicized priests to marry) and explains this on the basis of a papal indult that prohibits the exercise of orders. He does not explain how married Eastern rite clergy avoid being adulterous.

29. A scripture service without a homily presents as an ideal a cultic notion of worship that is inadequately related to life and mission. Without a homily, the scripture service is the dead husk of the liturgy of the word. Prohibiting lay preaching not only restricts lay ministry but also denies the laity's full membership in the Body of Christ.

30. See, for example, John J. Ziegler, *Let Them Anoint the Sick* (Collegeville: The Liturgical Press, 1987).

31. See my *The Reconciling Community* (Collegeville: The Liturgical Press, 1986), 117–18. For a fuller treatment, see Amédée Teetaert, *La Confession aux Laïques dans l'Église Latine* (Paris: Gabalda, 1926).

32. I have adapted this from Rahner, "Pastoral Ministries and Community Leadership," especially pp. 79–80.

33. The lack of the imposition of hands is not itself decisive: The church can and has changed the ritual for conferring office — the handing over of the signs of the office *(porrectio instrumentorum)* was once regarded as essential. Nor is the church's perception of sacramentality decisive: The fact that the sacramentality of episcopal ordination was disputed in the Middle Ages does not mean that it was not sacramental. What is decisive is the conferral of an office that touches the basic ecclesial reality of a faith community.

34. For an approach to ordination from a linguistic perspective, see L. William Countryman, *The Language of Ordination: Ministry in an Ecumenical Context* (Philadelphia: Trinity Press International, 1992).

35. GSF, nos. 3, 5, 6, 7, 14, 16, 17.

36. GSF, nos. 20, 21, 43.

37. GSF, nos. 32–33.

38. See "Priestless Parishes: Priests' Perspective," *Origins* 21 (1991): 41–53.

39. Although his research has been superseded, Joseph H. Fichter, *Religion as an Occupation: A Study in the Sociology of Professions* (Notre Dame, IN: University of Notre Dame Press, 1961), presented evidence more than thirty years ago that a disproportionate number of priests and religious had transcended the occupational level of their parents (p. 62). Although the decline in vocations had already begun, it received little attention. But Fichter did note that about two-thirds of the fathers were currently in white-collar professions, while only about thirty per cent had been so employed thirty years before, a sign of Catholic movement into the middle and upper classes (pp. 63–64). Because of social mobility, the church was having to depend more on white-collar families than on the working classes for vocations to the priesthood and religious life — and the numbers were no longer keeping pace with the growth of the Catholic population. There are signs that the church in developing and former Communist countries will have a similar experience.

40. See Arnold Angenendt and Thaddaeus A. Schnitker, "Die Privatmesse," *Liturgisches Jahrbuch* 33 (1983): 76–89; Otto Nussbaum, Kloster, *Priestermönch und Privatmesse: Ihr Verhältnis im Westen von den Anfängen bis zum hohen Mittelalter* (Bonn: Peter Hanstein, 1961); Angelus Albert Häussling, *Mönchskonvent und Eucharistiefeier: Eine Studie über die Messe in der abendländischen Klosterliturgie des frühen Mittelalters und zur Geschichte der Messhäufigkeit,* Liturgiewissenschaftliche Quellen und Forschungen, 58 (Münster: Aschendorffsche Verlagsbuchhandlung, 1971); Thomas P. Rausch, "Is the Private Mass Traditional?" *Worship* 64 (1990): 237–242; Edward Schillebeeckx, *The Church with a Human Face,* 159–160; Cyrille Vogel, "La multiplication des messes solitaires au moyen âge. Essai de statistique," *Revue des Sciences Religieuses* 55 (1981): 206–213; Cyrille Vogel, Une mutation cultuelle inexpliquée: Le passage de l'eucharistie communautaire a la messe privée," *Revue des Sciences Religieuses* 54 (1980): 230–250.

41. SC, no. 27.

42. GIRM, no. 211 [DOL 208, no. 1601].

43. Canon 906; see also canons 902 and 904.

44. John Paul II, "Address to the Roman Rota," (January 26, 1984), *Origins* 13 (1984), 584.

45. For recent discussions of stipends, see John M. Huels, "Stipends in the New Code of Canon Law," in R. Kevin Seasoltz, ed., *Living Bread, Saving Cup* (Collegeville: The Liturgical Press, 1987), 347–56; John M. Huels, "Mass Intentions," in *Disputed Questions in the Liturgy Today* (Chicago: Liturgy Training Publications, 1988), 47–55; Edward J. Kilmartin, "The Sacrifice of Thanksgiving and Social Justice," in Mark Searle, ed., *Liturgy and Social Justice* (Collegeville: The Liturgical Press, 1980), 53–71; M. Francis Mannion, "Stipends and Eucharistic Praxis," in R. Kevin Seasoltz, ed., *Living Bread, Saving Cup,* 324–46.

46. PO, no. 6.

The Implications for Catholic Spirituality of Sunday Worship in the Absence of a Priest

Decisions are now being made that will determine whether we will remain a sacramental church, centered on the word and the eucharist, or whether we will become a church centered on the word, with diminished sacramentality. This is being done at a time when Catholics are more involved in the eucharist than they have been for more than a millennium and when Protestant Christians are shifting to a balanced liturgy of word and sacrament. These decisions involve a willingness to tolerate the SWAP that takes place in many communities.

In both Catholicism and Protestantism, the twentieth-century liturgical movement and the subsequent liturgical reforms have had as their object the restoration of the classic pattern of the Sunday celebration of word and eucharist.[1] In Catholicism, this has required stripping away the accretions of the ages and returning the liturgy to the people through their active, intelligent participation as a community. In Protestantism, it has required restoring the sacramental celebration in which the word can be seen and handled (1 John 1:1), even tasted (Hebrews 6:4–5; 1 Peter 2:3), as well as heard. In both Catholicism and Protestantism, the recovery of the classic pattern of Sunday worship has meant once more recognizing the paschal or Easter mystery as the center of salvation history and experiencing it in celebration through rite and symbol.

Most Protestant traditions are still experiencing difficulty implementing the restoration of the eucharist as a regular part of Sunday worship. Transcending the medieval heritage of infrequent communion and the Reformation heritage of infrequent eucharist is not easy. Centuries of unfamiliarity have reduced the eucharist to a service occasionally appended to the liturgy of the word.

Catholicism has found the restoration relatively easy. The Tridentine reform of liturgy maintained the classic pattern of word and eucharist, and the gradual increase in the frequency of communion subsequent to Trent has reached a twentieth-century climax. Today the vast majority of those present at Sunday Mass participate in the celebration and share communion.

However, the SWAP that is now taking place in many communities — and which will become increasingly common in years to come — puts at risk the progress that has been made. Even the possibility of communion from the reserved sacrament is not enough to avoid the risk. As has happened in Protestantism with the eucharist, the communion service is likely to become an appendage to the word service. The eucharist, when it is celebrated, will be similarly perceived or will come to be regarded simply as the means for producing the consecrated hosts needed for the communion service.

What is at stake is more than a liturgical pattern consecrated by a constant tradition. The theological characteristics of this pattern translate into a spirituality, a way of life. This spirituality establishes the identity of the Catholic community and maintains its commitment to mission.

In analyzing the likely effects of SWAP on the church, we have examined the interrelationship of the eucharist and ecclesial communion, the difference between the eucharist as sacrifice and the communion service, and the significance of ordained ministry for a community. All of these are closely linked with sacramentality and the sacramental character of church, the very basis of Catholic spirituality. As a consequence, SWAP has implications for the Catholic sense of identity and mission, both of which flow from a sacramental spirituality.

That these implications are negative is hinted at in the Roman *Directory.* It refers to assemblies "in expectation of a priest" as hardly optimal (21) since the eucharistic sacrifice is "the only true actualization of the Lord's paschal mystery" and "the most complete manifestation of the church" (13). It also says that SWAP "should not take away but rather increase the desire of the faithful to take part in the celebration of the eucharist, and should make them more eager to be present at the celebration of the eucharist" (22). But it also gives the impression that, from the laity's perspective, the only difference is the priest's absence: The laity's involvement in the eucharistic sacrifice seems limited to receiving communion, and by receiving communion at SWAP they still receive the "fruits" of the sacrifice (32). The impression that the laity lose little in such celebrations is no evidence that absence will make the heart grow fonder. The *Directory* also gives hints of an awareness that local communities worshiping in this manner may grow away from their priest-pastors and the universal church.[2]

Gathered in Steadfast Faith, the statement of the U.S. Bishops on Sunday worship in the absence of a priest, is more forthright. It admits that the root problem, the lack of priests, remains unresolved (60, 63). It admits that SWAP may put both liturgical renewal and ecclesial communion at risk (21, 62). In stating the need to reflect upon the mystery of the church, the role of the baptized in the church's mission and the need to take new approaches to discerning vocations to the priesthood (3), the statement points delicately in the direction of resolving the root problem, which is, as we have seen, at its root ecclesiological rather than liturgical.

The frank admission in *Gathered in Steadfast Faith* of the existence of risks is the consequence of its broader understanding of both the relationship between the church and the liturgy and between the assembly and the priest. Unlike the *Directory,* it emphasizes the common priesthood of the baptized (3, 5, 6, 27, 61) and regards the eucharist and all liturgy as the action of the assembly (6, 16, 17, 23, 24, 48). It is clearer on the nature of the ordained ministry (25, 26), and it emphasizes the role of the eucharist in maintaining identity and sustaining mission (3, 7, 21, 43). *Gathered in Steadfast Faith* also stresses the various modes of Christ's presence (7, 22–25, 28) and the essential notion of sacramentality (7). The relationship of the eucharist and Sunday is also clearer than in the *Directory* (7, 10–17).

Even more significantly, *Gathered in Steadfast Faith* pays attention to the ways in which the eucharist does what SWAP cannot. The eucharist proclaims the paschal mystery (16, 18, 40–43); the eucharist is the font and summit of the church's life (7); the church recognizes and expresses itself in the eucharist (8, 12, 16, 19, 20); and the eucharist strengthens the bonds of communion (16, 17, 28). *Gathered in Steadfast Faith* does not speak of sacrifice directly as often as the *Directory* does (8, 58), but it does speak often of the eucharist as an action (6, 8, 14, 16, 17) and of responsibility for mission (3, 5, 6, 7, 14, 16, 17). It also stresses that the local assembly is a focus for broader life and ministry (20, 21, 43).

Gathered in Steadfast Faith, like the *Directory,* expresses the hope that good celebrations of SWAP will encourage communities to look forward to the celebration of the eucharist (8, 20). Its general mood, however, though more positive and optimistic than the *Directory,* betrays a sense of frustration that the real issues are being ignored. Perhaps because it is more forthright than the *Directory,* it highlights the need to face serious theological questions. Its framers appear to have realized that SWAP is an attempt to provide a liturgical solution to an ecclesiological problem.

Clearly, some aspects of the ecclesiology and liturgical theology of Vatican II can still be expressed and effected in SWAP. Nevertheless, the central element of communion will be diminished and distorted because of the elements of the eucharist that are absent from SWAP. In particular, the inability to share in proclaiming and celebrating the paschal mystery — Christ's redemptive sacrifice — will keep communities immature and dependent in relation to the broader church and will perpetuate a devotional approach to the eucharist.

The sacraments of baptism and eucharist are closely linked with community and the Lord's Day. Sunday, assembly and the eucharist are so interrelated that it is hard to imagine how people could possibly remain Christian without them. Certainly individuals can, because of the Spirit's action; but the action of the Spirit will not be experienced in a human, sacramental way in a community's life. Nor will such communities experience themselves as a living part of the Catholic sacramental tradition, with responsibility for that tradition. The tradition links the Lord's Day, the local gathered church and the celebration of the eucharist. It insists that celebrating the eucharist on the Lord's Day is an essential part of the community's identity as the Body of Christ.

The reason, of course, is that the eucharist is the memorial of the paschal mystery. In the celebration of the eucharist, Christians are gathered by the Spirit as Christ's Body to give thanks to God. They give thanks for what God has accomplished through the Word made human by the power of the Spirit. They especially give thanks for the liberating love of God revealed by the Spirit in Jesus' being raised from death to life as head of his Body, the church. In the memorial, they experience anew the action of God in the Spirit making them Christ's Body. They are empowered for a mission that will come to completion in the ultimate divine renewal of the cosmos in the likeness of Christ.

So important is this that I must disagree with Schillebeeckx and others who argue that a local community has such a right to the eucharist that it may provide its own leaders if the wider church does not provide an ordained presider.[3] The local community has no *right* to the eucharist: It has the *duty* and the *responsibility* to celebrate the eucharist on the Lord's Day because in no other way can its members experience their identity and mission so powerfully. Jesus did not say, "You *may* do this as my memorial if you want." He said, "*Do* this as my memorial." It is not that communities unable to celebrate the eucharist are merely deprived of a "right." Rather, it is that they are kept from being faithfully obedient to the mandate of Christ. Their identity is imperiled and their participation in mission risks being distorted. But to remedy the situation by having communities provide presiders for themselves would mean schism, the breaking of communion. The dilemma is obvious.

The central issue is thus misnamed. The issue to be addressed is not Sundays without priests but Sunday assemblies without the eucharist. Providing for Sunday assemblies with a lay presider risks destroying the intimate link between the assembly and the eucharist. The real problem is ignored, namely, that the failure to recognize through ordination the role of those who exercise pastoral leadership in a community deprives communities of the eucharist.

Increasingly, communities will be gathering for Sunday worship and listening together to the word of God, but they will not be sharing the action of God in the eucharist because their worship leaders are not ordained. As churches in the Reformation tradition have been rediscovering during this century, the liturgy of the word is not an adequate form of Sunday worship independent of the eucharist, to which it is oriented and which is the initial, orienting response to the word.

Granted, communities will, when possible, be dining together on what is left over from a previous eucharist. But they will not be celebrating the eucharist. And, as the Body of Christ, they have the responsibility to do so. They must experience who they are, not just preserve a memory.

They may do their best to maintain the attitude of the eucharist. They will remember the action of God in Christ and respond in praise and thanksgiving. But remembering is not the same as the real experience. We must not reach the point where we are satisfied with a communion service. The eucharist is much more than the Lord's presence in consecrated bread and wine: It is the celebration of the Easter mystery, the Lord's dying and rising. We cannot fully be the Body of Christ without that experience.

There can, of course, be worship without the eucharist. Other forms of sharing God's action in Christ flow from the eucharist and lead back to it. They complement the eucharist by enabling us to concentrate on particular aspects of the Easter mystery. We do need to recover from "monoeucharistitis," as John Baldovin has diagnosed the malady caused by limiting the church's worship to only the eucharist. However, none of the liturgical complements to eucharist can substitute for it.

When they are used, these other forms of worship must also provide an experience of sharing God's action in Christ. This is especially the case when another form of worship is all that a community has available for its Sunday gathering. To approximate the eucharist, the community should at least share in blessing God, in offering God the service of praise and thanksgiving. That is why a prayer of thanksgiving is mentioned in the *Directory* (41, 45) and why many rituals provide forms for it. Yet this attempt to compensate for what is missing, far from increasing the desire for the eucharist, is likely instead to dull the appetite.

It is questionable whether we can maintain our identity as a sacramental church, a eucharistic church, without the Sunday celebration of both word and sacrament. Luke 24:13 – 35 presents the basic pattern of Christian community: being formed by the word, recognizing Christ in the breaking of bread and going forth on its mission. That pattern has remained constant, even in eras when participation was limited and the assembly was not the celebrant of the eucharist. The blurred lines of that pattern have become clearer over the last century and Catholic Christians have come to a new awareness of their identity and mission.

Some Practical Concerns

Unfortunately, the issue of "priestless Sundays" is rarely addressed publicly from the perspective of what its impact on Catholic spirituality is likely to be. The attempt is merely to continue business as usual — but without the eucharist — without considering what will be the consequence. In addition to the theological issues mentioned earlier, several practical problems surround the Sunday celebration with a lay presider.

(1) *Confusion with the Mass.* The fact that the format of SWAP so closely follows that of the Mass can easily lead to the statement, "I like it better when Sister says Mass." Of course, the difficulty of distinguishing the two also says something about the quality of our eucharistic celebrations and how they are experienced! Catechesis, though necessary, can go only so far in preventing or remedying the confusion. We must improve the quality of all liturgical celebration as the action of the assembled community.

(2) *Liturgy that is verbal and verbose.* This is often the case
with the celebration of the Mass, of course. We rely upon
words — whose primary appeal is to the intellect — rather than
on the nonverbal symbols that engage us at a deeper, more primal and more holistic and encompassing level. Even with a
communion service, SWAP will intensify this reliance on words.
For example, in the Canadian *Ritual for Lay Presiders,* the lay
presider verbally states communion with the priest-pastor and
with the bishop and the wider church. The *Directory* also suggests this practice (42). Words substitute for sacrament! The non-
eucharistic service must give special attention to symbols or it
will seem more like reading a menu than sharing a meal, especially since the meal is one of consecrated bread from another
celebration. For different reasons and in a different manner,
we are repeating the mistake of the Protestant reformers: The
"Protestant mind became fascinated with words rather than
symbols [and] shifted from a culture of imagery to a culture
of words."[4]

(3) *Loss of appreciation for eucharistic celebration.* This will be
the case if the lay-led noneucharistic celebration is done too
well and thus becomes more attractive, if it is shorter, if it
becomes common or if the Mass comes to be regarded as simply the means of producing consecrated hosts for the communion service. The sense of self-sufficiency generated by sole
responsibility for Sunday worship can lead to resentment when
a sacramental minister from outside the community comes
in for Mass: The eucharist seems to be imposed upon the
community. Lack of familiarity may lead to distaste. Or, simply,
the rarity of the eucharist may dull the appetite and lead to
eucharistic anorexia.

(4) *Inadequate and ineffective celebrations.* If, at least initially,
lay-led noneucharistic celebrations are more attractive, it will be
due to the inadequacy and ineffectiveness of the present celebrations of the eucharist. But will SWAP be able to maintain the
vibrancy and vitality that makes it initially attractive? The long-
range likelihood is that lay leaders of worship are likely to
copy what they are used to, and SWAP will begin to suffer from
the same inadequacies that hinder effective celebrations of
the Mass.

(5) *Non-attendance.* It may be the case that, if possible, people will go to Mass elsewhere, join another church or simply

cease worshiping regularly. The community diminished by loss of membership will suffer a loss of vitality as a consequence. What will happen to our sense of local church?

(6) *Broader ministry in/to the community.* The faith-community is not simply a worshiping community. If the community has no stable ministry to coordinate its life together, individualistic patterns and a service-station approach to church, community and the eucharist will be reinforced. Lay pastoral ministers can undoubtedly compensate for this to a great extent, as is already evident in the parishes — even those with priests — where they are serving. But can they provide the motivation and empowerment that the eucharist, the experience of the Easter mystery, gives?

The Need for Catechesis

These problems all show the need for catechesis on several points or issues, as well as a deeper appreciation of how they are formative of Christian spirituality:

(1) *The primacy of Sunday.* Sunday worship has a primacy that has been obscured by the frequent celebration of weekday Mass and by a lack of knowledge of the rhythms of liturgical time. The failure to recognize the primacy of Sunday is evident in the suggestion that the "Sunday obligation" be transferred to a day when it is possible for the priest to be present. But it is on the Lord's Day that the community is to gather and show what it is called to be — the Body of Christ.

(2) *The primacy of the local community and its eucharistic assembly.* We often fail to experience and understand that it is the Body of Christ that celebrates the eucharist. The gathered local community presents itself sacramentally as the Body of Christ. Even when the community lacks a priest presider, its gathering for worship is more significant than individuals traveling elsewhere for Mass. This is not recognized by the *Directory,* which recommends going elsewhere for Mass if that is possible (18).

(3) *The role of the priest presider and the lay presider.* The priest's role in the eucharist needs to be clarified. The significance of the priest's presence is sacramental and cannot be reduced to a power to consecrate. Catechesis should clarify the sacramental role and function of the priest, the priest's relationship to the community and the community's relationship to the priest. It should also clarify what the role of a lay leader of prayer is supposed to be and the relationship between the lay presider and the community. Ideally, the one who presides should have a broader relationship to the community than a liturgical one.

(4) *Eucharist and communion service.* Catechesis should also explore the relationship between the eucharist and the communion service and how they differ from one another. There are serious issues here: If the Sunday liturgy of the word and the communion service become common, what does this say about the meaning of the eucharist? Should communion be shared outside Mass? Will people come if there is no communion service? What does the difficulty people have in distinguishing the communion service from the eucharist say about the quality of our eucharistic celebrations?

Conclusion

The lack of priests makes SWAP necessary. Catholics come every Sunday to the Lord's table, but in many parishes there is no priest to lead the table prayer and no Supper to share. The severity of the problem varies by area, but it is true everywhere that priests ordained to preside at the Lord's table become fewer and older as the Catholic community becomes larger. At root, the problem is the lack of priests, and "to offer a liturgical solution to a non-liturgical problem"[5] is unwise, to say the least.

Jesus' command to his disciples was, "*Do* this in memory of me"; not "*Say* this," "*Look* at this," or "*Receive* this." The eucharist is first of all an action. It is the action of Jesus in praise and thanksgiving, dedicating himself to the service of all by offering himself to the God who identifies himself with humanity. It is, at the same time, the action of Christ as the church, identifying us with himself in his self-offering as we take bread and cup, bless God, and share his table. In that way, Jesus makes us his Body and shapes us in his image.

The church in its form as local assembly is the Body of Christ. The eucharist is the celebration of the Body of Christ wherein it recognizes and realizes its identity and mission. That is why the church has not merely a right to the eucharist but the responsibility to celebrate it on the Lord's Day. Communities thus have a right to have ministers presiding at their table who are signs of their ecclesial reality and communion with the Catholic church. Without that celebration, Catholicism can survive only as an inflexible institution, a defective sacrament of Christ's nourishing Body — a stone, rather than bread for the world, because it has consciously chosen to ignore the commission Christ gave to his disciples.

A choice is presently being made regarding the shape of the future church. Simply continuing the present policy is a choice, and it is one that is a more radical departure from tradition than changing the ordination discipline. It necessarily means the diminishment of a church that has always given pride of place to expressing its sacramental character in celebrating the eucharist. Catholicism could cease to be a catholic, sacramental, eucharistic church. Do we dare risk losing the sacramental consciousness that is key to recognizing God in Christ and in life? "For Christians to give up their sacramental sense would be like language giving up metaphor: either surrender would mean that whole areas of reality could no longer be given voice."[6]

Admittedly, until recently, the church's eucharistic focus was more on the reserved sacrament than on the celebration. Although recent shifts have reoriented both theology and practice, the reorientation is too recent to be firmly rooted. As a consequence, communion from the reserved sacrament seems sufficiently eucharistic to be acceptable as a substitute. But it is not. People — the Church — receive something less for their nourishment than they need in order to remain fully the Body of Christ serving the world.

Chapter Six
Endnotes

1. For an analysis of this process and its theological advantages, see Geoffrey Wainwright, "Renewing Worship: The Recovery of Classical Patterns," *Theology Today* 48 (1991): 45–55.

2. It often speaks of the need for catechesis, and requires that the assembly be urged to unite in spirit with the community with whom the pastor is celebrating eucharist (42).

3. See Edward Schillebeeckx, ed., "The Right of a Community to a Priest," *Concilium* 133 (1980).

4. John M. Mulder, "Symbols as Teachers," *Theology Today* 42 (1985): 191.

5. Marrevée, " 'Priestless Masses,' " 219.

6. Kavanagh, "Liturgy and Ecclesial Consciousness," 13.

INDEX